Battlefields of Canada

Mary Beacock Fryer

Toronto and Reading
Dundurn Press
1986

Design and Production: Andy Tong
Typesetting: Typografix Inc.
Printing and Binding: Hignell Printing Limited, Winnipeg, Canada

The writing of this manuscript and the publication of this book were made possible by support from several sources. The publisher wishes to acknowledge the generous assistance and ongoing support of The Canada Council and The Ontario Arts Council.
   Care has been taken to trace the ownership of copyright material used in the text (including the illustrations). The author and publisher welcome any information enabling them to rectify any reference or credit in subsequent editions.

J. Kirk Howard, Publisher

Canadian Cataloguing in Publication Data

Fryer, Mary Beacock, 1929-
   Battlefields of Canada

Bibliography: p.
Includes index.
ISBN 1-55002-007-2

1. Battlefields - Canada. 2. Battles - Canada.
3. Canada - History, Military. I. Title.

FC226.F79 1986   971   C86-094666-5
F1028.F76 1986

Second Printing: February 1995

Dundurn Press Limited   Dundurn Distribution   Dundurn Press Limited
2181 Queen Street East   73 Lime Walk   1823 Maryland Avenue
Suite 301   Headington, Oxford   P.O. Box 1000
Toronto, Canada   England   Niagara Falls, N.Y.
M4E 1E5   OX3 7AD   U.S.A. 14302-1000

Battlefields of Canada

Mary Beacock Fryer

CONTENTS

Acknowledgements

The author and publisher wish to thank the following for their informed comments on various chapters: Mrs Ann Boyer, Curator, Battlefield House, Stoney Creek, Ontario; Mr James Candow, Parks Canada, Signal Hill National Park; Mr Dennis Carter-Edwards, Research Historian, Ontario Region, Parks Canada; Mr D.J. Delaney, Area Superintendent, Fort Wellington National Historic Park, Prescott, Ontario; Mr. Michel Filteau, P.H.N. Les fortifications de Quebec, ville de Quebec, Quebec; Mr Daniel J. Glenney and Mr Walter Haldorson, Niagara National Historic Parks, Niagara-on-the-Lake, Ontario; Mme. Michelle Guitard, historian, ville de Quebec, Quebec; Mr Willian Naftel, Acting Chief, Historical Resources Research, Parks Canada, Atlantic Region, Halifax, Nova Scotia; Mr S.C. Ridlington, Area Interpretation Officer, Fort Beauséjour, National Historic Park, Aulac, New Brunswick; Ms Barbara Schmeisser, Project Historian, Fort Beauséjour National Historic Park, Aulac, New Brunswick; Mrs Elinor Kyte Senior, historian, Montreal, Quebec; Dr Hereward Senior, historian, Montreal, Quebec; Captain C.H. Shaw (N) Ret'd, Director, Maritime Museum of British Columbia, Victoria, British Columbia. In addition we wish to thank Dr. W.A.B. Douglas, Directorate of History, Department of National Defence; Fred Gaffen, Canadian War Museum; Terence B. Smythe, Historical Research Division, National Historic Parks and Sites, Parks Canada, and Rex Williams, Cariad, whose idea this book was; and Barbara Fryer, who helped with the proofreading.

Introduction

The Oxford Dictionary defines a battle as a fight, especially between large forces. By that judgement, Canada has only four real battlefields – Louisbourg in 1745 and 1758, Quebec because of the battles fought there in 1759 and 1760, the Richelieu River-Lake Champlain corridor from the era of New France until 1813, and the Niagara peninsula in 1812-1814. Most of the serious battles were fought in these places. The fights that occurred in the rest of the country were hardly more than skirmishes, defined in the Dictionary as irregular or unpremeditated fighting, especially between small or outlying parties, or as small engagements. At the same time, a skirmish fulfilled another criterion for a battle, that of resistance. Without opposition an attack was really a raid, or surprise predatory incursion. If Canada is short of battlefields, especially in the west, there is no dearth of skirmishes or raids.

The battlefields included in this book have been selected for various reasons – importance, scale, special features, comic or bizarre aspects, historical epoch, or regional distribution. Describing in this book battlefields exclusively from Nova Scotia, Quebec and Ontario would have restricted both scope and interest. Alberta is lucky in having only one site –Frenchman's Butte, which in 1885 was the setting for what really amounted to a skirmish. Prince Edward Island has no battlefield, but certain raids were a consequences of its link to Louisbourg.

Other criteria for selection were accessibility and state of preservation. Where a battlefield has been set aside as a national or provincial historic site, there is something to see, something resembling the location at the time of the battle. In other instances the site has been so altered that it is no longer possible to see what actually happened. Lundy's Lane on the Niagara peninsula, for example, was the site of a bloody, sustained, indecisive battle in 1814, but the site has been built upon and the scene is difficult to envisage. Queenston Heights, in the same area, is a public park, preserved as open space, where a visitor can easily see what happened. One battlefield left out, with regret, is the Long Sault of the Ottawa River, where Dollard des Ormeaux made his stand against the Iroquois. Historians and archaeologists can not agree on the location of the site.

Not all battlefields selected are historic sites. One setting that invites exploration is that of the Battle of the Thousand Islands, fought in 1760. Tracing the events involves locations, both public and private, in both Ontario and New York State which can be visited by boat. And this battle site is not the only instance where the present boundary between Canada and United States has been ignored in the selection of the following battlefields. Many sites not in Canada are the setting for battles that affected this country. One such is Carillon-Ticonderoga. This site was of such strategic importance that, although in New York State, it has been included in this collection.

A chronology in the appendix provides a more complete record of all the disturbances that have taken place in Canada from the arrival of the first Europeans, and it also pinpoints some sites where native peoples fought battles that did not involve Europeans. This list fills in the gaps inevitably made by the selection of 16 battlefields, and helps place these battles in their wider context.

Early Exploration and Settlement

Champlain's battle against the Iroquois near Ticonderoga in 1609. Behind the French officer are his Huron and Algonquin allies.

The story of the first Europeans in central Canada is the story of the struggle to control the fur trade. To any European furs were a great bargain. Although some items exchanged for furs were useful, such as knives, axes, kettles and cloth, many were cheap trinkets, or liquor, which did unpardonable harm to native people unaccustomed to it. The European appetite for furs was insatiable, and the quest to find new areas where animals were plentiful led to the exploration of more and more of the interior.

In the process the natives developed such an appetite for trade goods that competing European powers were able to form alliances with individual nations or tribes to keep the Indians divided. United, they might have been able to preserve their territories and way of life much longer. The natives helped the newcomers by showing them how to live as they did; otherwise the interlopers would not have taken control of the country so easily. European penetration of the interior was done with native cooperation. The destruction of Huronia — the land of the Huron Indians — came about as a consequence of these alliances and rivalries.

New France began in 1608 when Samuel de Champlain founded his little settlement of traders at Quebec, choosing the site for its defence possibilities. If the French were to survive they needed allies. Champlain was quick to perceive the disunity that prevailed among the different nations. By accompanying some Huron and Algonquin warriors to attack the Iroquois in the vicinity of Lake Champlain in 1609, Champlain committed France to an alliance with these nations. Henceforth the warriors of the five Iroquois nations — Mohawks, Oneidas, Onondagas, Cayugas and Senecas — were France's enemies despite certain successes when the French lured some Iroquois close to Montreal to live. The real losers in the struggle between France and the Iroquois were the Hurons.

Huronia 1600s

The Hurons and the Iroquois shared an Iroquoian language, and their longhouses in stockaded villages, and the fields where corn, beans and squash were grown on mounds were similar. Otherwise they were rivals who had fought each other long before the arrival of Europeans — a rivalry that the Dutch and French, and later the English, could exploit.

Huronia, the country of the four nations that made up the Huron, or Wendat, Confederacy, lay between Lake Simcoe and the shores of Georgian Bay. The Hurons, whose numbers have been estimated as 16,000 at the time of their first contact with Europeans, were a trading people. Their own country, where they practiced their shifting agriculture and lived in some eighteen villages, was not rich in beaver. They traded with tribes farther afield and sold pelts to French traders. The members of the Iroquois Confederacy, whose tribal lands lay south of the Great Lakes, had a similar trading rela-

Ste. Marie Among the Hurons, an overview. This oblique artist's representation shows the extent of the Jesuit headquarters in Huronia.

Huronia

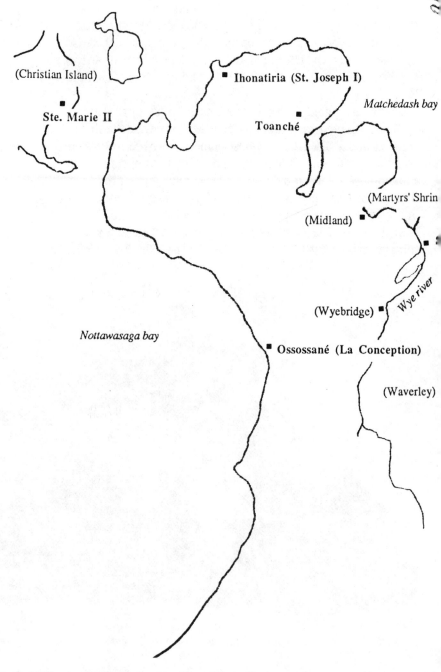

(Christian Island)

Ste. Marie II

Ihonatiria (St. Joseph I)

Matchedash bay

Toanché

(Martyrs' Shrin

(Midland)

Wye river

(Wyebridge)

Nottawasaga bay

Ossossané (La Conception)

(Waverley)

Huronia in the 1600s, showing the relationship of some Huron villages to modern communities.

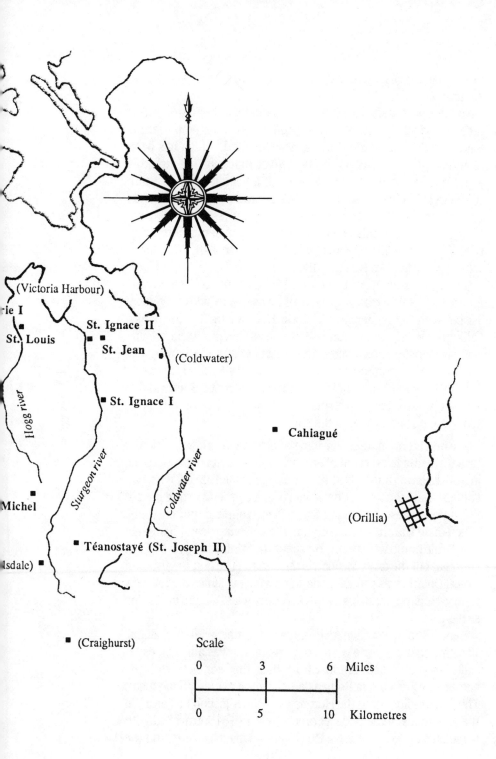

(Victoria Harbour)

rie I

St. Louis

St. Ignace II

St. Jean

(Coldwater)

Hogg river

St. Ignace I

Cahiagué

Sturgeon river

Coldwater river

Michel

(Orillia)

Téanostayé (St. Joseph II)

lsdale)

(Craighurst)

Scale

0	3	6	Miles
0	5	10	Kilometres

17

tionship with the Dutch in the 1600s, when they had a fur fort at Albany.

No one specific site can be called a battlefield, but a number of archaeological sites have been identified. The most important is Sainte Marie among the Hurons, near Midland, which has been restored, even to locks on the Wye River that runs through this Jesuit mission to the Huron people. At a visitors' centre a film recreates life in the mission. Above Sainte Marie on the hill stands the Shrine, built to commemorate the six priests and two lay brothers who were killed by the Iroqouois. More of the Huron way of life is shown at the Huronia Museum and a reconstructed Huron village in Little Lake Park, Midland.

Four other sites have been identified and marked. One is St. Ignace II. A plaque marking the site is on the south side of Highway 12 between Coldwater and Victoria Harbour in Tay Township. Cahiagué, an important Huron village, has been partly excavated, near Warminster, fifteen kilometres west of Orillia off Highway 12. A marker in Victoria Harbour commemrates the St. Louis mission; the site is about three kilometres up the Hogg River. Sainte Marie II is on Christian Island, the marker on the east side of the island above the bay and close to the shore.

The first Frenchman to live in what is now Ontario was Etienne Brulé, a teen-aged servant of Samuel de Champlain. At Tadoussac in 1609, New France's first governor met some Hurons who had come to trade their furs. Champlain decided to send young men to live among these natives to learn their language and customs. When more Hurons came with furs the following year, Champlain sent Brulé home with them. He spent the winter of 1610-1611 in Huronia, but the exact location is uncertain. (The first Englishman to visit Ontario was spending the same winter in James Bay. He was Henry Hudson, and his ship *Discovery* was frozen in for the season.)

Trade was a powerful motive for having contact with the Indians. The propagation of the gospel of Christianity was another, especially for the French. Almost from their first contacts with the natives, the French sent Roman Catholic missionaries among them. The first missionary to the Hurons was Father Joseph Le Caron, in the grey robes of the Récollet order, who, in 1615, travelled with some guides up the Ottawa River, along Lake Nipissing and the

French River to Lake Huron, thence to Huronia. Not many days later Champlain followed the same route, accompanied by some Frenchmen and native guides. In Huronia he found that a large war party was forming at Cahiagué to go to attack the Iroquois in their own country. Impressed by the Frenchmen's 'fire sticks' the warriors asked Champlain and his men to accompany them, and the governor agreed.

South of Huronia was the country of the Petuns, and along Lake Erie that of the Neutrals. Like the Hurons and Iroquois, the Petuns and the Neutrals spoke an Iroquoian language. The latter two tried to avoid the rivalry that existed between the Wendat and Iroquois Confederacies. The war party Champlain and his men accompanied travelled by canoe through the Kawartha Lakes and the Trent River to Lake Ontario, and from there they ascended the Oswego River into the country of the Oneidas. The Hurons were defeated and

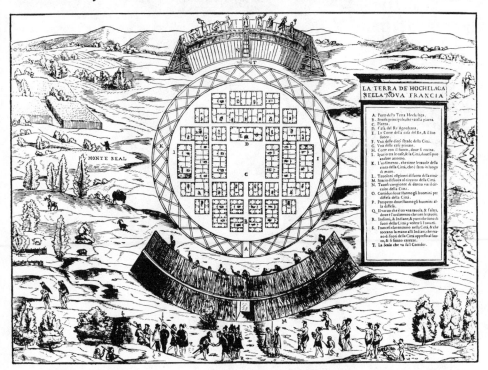

Plan of Hochelaga (Montreal) in the 16th century by Giovanni Ramusio, shown in an Italian translation of Cartier's Voyages. *It was based on Cartier's descriptions and may not be very accurate.*

forced to withdraw. Champlain received an arrow in the leg and was taken back to the Huron country to recuperate. When he returned to Quebec the following year, Father Le Caron went with him.

For a time the French missionaries concentrated their efforts at conversion among the tribes of the eastern woodlands — nomadic hunters who were not easy to find. Hoping for better luck with natives who lived in more permanent agricultural villages, the Missionaries turned their attention to Huronia. Several Récollets

Huron warrior wearing slat armour, from Champlain's Voyages *of 1619.*

went there, and more of Champlain's young men joined Etienne Brulé.

The Récollets were a very poor order, lacking the money for an effective mission, and consequently, they invited the wealthy Jesuit order to join them. The first black-robed Jesuits arrived in Quebec in 1625. At that time the Récollet, Nicolas Viel, living in a cabin at the Huron village of Toanaché, on the west shore of Penetanguishene Bay, was exhausted. He set out for Quebec to have a rest, but his canoe was swamped in the rapids near the Island of Montreal and he drowned.

In 1626 three priests went westwards – the Récollet La Roche de Daillon, and Jesuits Jean de Brébeuf and Anne de Nouë. They occupied Father Viel's cabin at Toanché, where Brébeuf remained for three years. The other two left in 1628.

In 1629, Captain David Kirke was sent with three ships to Quebec to capture the stronghold for England. Etienne Brulé and Nicolas Marsolet went to pilot in a French fleet Champlain was expecting.

View of the restored Ste.-Marie Among the Hurons from the Wye River.

Instead, Brulé and Marsolet met Kirke's ships at Tadoussac and agreed to guide them into Quebec's harbour. Champlain surrendered, and Kirke sent the governor and all the missionaries back to France. Three years later, in 1632, by the Treaty of St. Germain-en-Laye, Canada was returned to France. Etienne Brulé, living at Toanché, was murdered by the Hurons, who feared Champlain's wrath if he caught them sheltering the turncoat. Thus ended the life of the first Frenchman to explore Ontario.

Champlain returned from France, accompanied by black-robed Jesuits but no Récollets, for economy reasons. The Jesuits could pay their own way. In 1634 the Jesuit Fathers, Jean de Brébeuf, Antoine Daniel and Ambroise Davost, with some hired men, went to Huronia. At Ihonatiria, near the northern tip of the Penetanguishene peninsula, they started a mission named St. Joseph.

During the 1635 growing season, both drought and disease struck Ihonatiria, and the survivors left the village. When new Jesuits arrived, Brébeuf moved to the village of Ossossané on Nottawasaga Bay, and opened a new mission, La Conception de Notre Dame. In 1637, Father Jérôme Lalemant opened another mission, St. Joseph II, at Teanaustayé on the upper reaches of the Sturgeon River.

Seeing the need for a well-fortified, centrally-located mission, Lalemant built Sainte Marie (now restored) on the shore of Wye River. His workmen opened the first canal in central Canada, with three small locks to divert water within the stockade of Sainte Marie. The Hurons began to trust the missionaries but these were also years when new diseases swept the country. The well-meaning priests and their helpers, all unaware, were the cause of these misfortunes. Measles and smallpox, introduced by Europeans, took a fearful toll despite the efforts of the missionaries to care for the sick.

In the 1640s, when the Hurons had been weakened by disease, the Iroquois saw their opportunity to end the threat posed by the Wendat-French alliance, and to gain control of the fur trade for themselves. Both native confederacies wanted the fire sticks but the French were reluctant to trade such weapons. The Dutch had no such scruples, and they supplied their Iroquois allies with muskets and ammunition. In 1642 the Iroquois attacked the Huron village of Contarea, near the shore of Lake Simcoe (south of Orillia),

Martyrdom of Brébeuf and Lalemant, March 1649. Europeans could be equally cruel in executing those they considered guilty of crimes.

killed everyone they found, and put the settlement to the torch. Next, they isolated the Hurons by occupying lands along the Ottawa River that belonged to the Algonquin tribe, cutting off communication with Quebec for months, since they also had villages close to the St. Lawrence.

In 1645, Father Jérôme Lalemant left Huronia and the new Superior was Father Paul Ragueneau, who was based at Sainte Marie. By that time the Jesuits had fifty-eight men in Huronia — twenty-two soldiers, eighteen priests, the rest engagés who were allowed to earn money trading, or donnés who were unpaid volunteers. The Jesuits had opened a dozen missions, nine to the Hurons, and three among the Petuns and Algonquins. Land around

Sainte Marie had been planted with crops so that the Black Robes, as the Hurons called them, could feed the hundreds who visited them.

The first of the Jesuit martyrs met their fate in 1646. Emboldened by their success in Huronia, the Jesuits attempted to found a mission to the Iroquois. They chose Father Isaac Joques, who had been in Huronia but was then on the Island of Montreal, to go into the Mohawk Valley. In late August, Father Joques set out, accompanied by a lay brother, Jean de Lalande. The Mohawks killed them, placed their heads on a palisade, and threw their bodies into the Mohawk River.

At Teanaustayé, Father Antoine Daniel was in charge of St. Joseph II mission. On 4 July 1648, the Iroquois attacked, and Father Daniel was among those killed. On 14 March 1649, they struck the mission of St. Ignace, on a tributary of the Coldwater River. Hurons fleeing from St. Ignace stopped at St. Louis mission, to the west, to warn the two missionaries then living there, Fathers Jean de Brébeuf and Gabriel Lalement (a nephew of Father Jérôme Lalement). The two priests refused to desert their flock at St. Louis and both were subsequently tortured to death. Word reached Sainte Marie, where Father Ragueneau decided to evacuate the mission. A war party of Hurons headed for St. Louis mission (on the Hogg River south of Victoria Harbour) to try and turn back the Iroquois. They fought furiously while Father Ragueneau and his followers burned Sainte Marie. The black robes and some Hurons headed for Christian Island for safety, and there they started a second Sainte Marie.

While the destitute Hurons fled to the new Sainte Marie for succour, the Iroquois attacked the three missions to the Petun and Algonquin Indians, and they killed Fathers Charles Garnier and Nöel Chabanel. At Sainte Marie II, the winter was exceedingly severe, for there was not enough food on the island for all the refugee Hurons. In the spring Father Ragueneau evacuated the mission, and with about sixty Frenchmen and 300 Hurons, he set off in canoes for Quebec. The Jesuits' plan for Huronia had ended in flames at the hands of the Iroquois.

Now the Iroquois turned on the rest of the Petuns, and on the Neutrals, killing them and driving the survivors west and south; later they regrouped and called themselves Wyandots. When the warriors of the Iroquois Confederacy returned to their own country deep inside New York State, the lands of their fellow-Iroquoians lay desolate and deserted. Gradually the Mississaugas, who spoke an Algonkian language, drifted southwards and hunted through the once fertile fields.

In 1664, England wrested the colony of New Netherlands from the Dutch and renamed it New York. The change only intensified the rivalry over the fur trade, and convinced the French to move farther inland. As beaver disappeared from one area through over-trapping, explorers moved on in search of new territory where the animal was still plentiful. As the fur traders moved on towards the west, so did the missionaries, until Britain finally succeeded in acquiring New France slightly more than a century after the demise of the Jesuit missions to Huronia.

The French-British Conflict

Taking of Quebec in 1629. This fanciful representation was published in 1689 in an account of the explorations of Father Louis Hennepin.

The final contest between Britain and France in North America was part of the Seven Years' War – the North American phase of which has been known as the French and Indian War. The Seven Years' War began in 1756 and ended in 1763 when the peace treaty was signed. The French and Indian War really began in 1754 and ended in 1760. In fact, tension had remained high, almost unabated, since the signing of the treaty of Utrecht in 1713. Under its terms, all of Acadia had been ceded to Britain. France hoped to be able to retain the part that is now New Brunswick by guarding the Isthmus of Chignecto, thereby confining British settlement to pennisular Nova Scotia.

From 1744 to 1748, Britain and France were on opposite sides in the War of the Austrian Succession, which spread to both countries' colonies as King George's War. At that time the merchants of Massachusetts were worried over depredations against their shipping by French privateers operating from Louisbourg. Thus in 1745 they launched their unlikely expedition that captured the great fortress on Cape Breton Island.

The Treaty of Aix-la-Chapelle in 1748 ended the war on both continents and brought some respite. Then matters came to a head over the ownership of the Ohio Valley, which both Britain and France claimed. Britain's Thirteen Colonies wanted room for expansion. France was already at work on a chain of posts to link the Great Lakes to Louisiana, her colony at the mouth of the Mississippi River. Armed conflict began in 1754, two years before the formal declaration of war, when a small expedition led by a Virginia colonel, George Washington, was defeated at Fort Necessity by a French force from Fort Duquesne (the site of Pittsburgh, Pennsylvania).

Afterwards the war was fought on three fronts – in the Ohio country and near Lake Erie; through the Gulf of St. Lawrence and the lower part of that river; and on the long-standing warpath along the Richelieu-Champlain-Hudson waterway. Still standing as through it is guarding that route of easy access is the restored Fort Ticonderoga (built by the French as Fort Carillon). The battlefield is in New York State, yet its story belongs as much to Canada as to the United States. Ticonderoga, and Crown Point a short distance north of it where the French built Fort St. Frédéric, are two of many sites that both countries share.

Because of the importance of the Seven Years' War era for the development of modern Canada, six of the battlefields are described in this book. In scope and consequences, this war overshadows all other conflicts. The War of 1812, by comparison, was a minor affair fought by smaller armies. Nothing in the later war matched the size of the armies that faced each other at Louisbourg, Carillon, and Quebec.

Following the humiliating defeat at Fort Necessity, in July 1755, the British commander-in-chief, General Edward Braddock, led an expedition against Fort Duquesne. He was ambushed and defeated by the French and their Indian allies. That September a British force defeated the French on Lake George, but it failed in its objective of capturing Fort St. Frédéric at Crown Point. In the east the British captured Fort Beauséjour in June and expelled the Acadians from the neighbourhood. That autumn the British began building Fort William Henry at the foot of Lake George, and Fort Edward on the upper Hudson River. The French started work on Fort Carillon on the Ticonderoga peninsula.

Britain formally declared war on France on 17 May 1756. Montcalm, the new French commander-in-chief, captured the forts at the mouth of the Oswego River in August and destroyed them. The following August, in 1757, Montcalm captured Fort William Henry. By 1758 the British were ready for successes, because of the determination of the new Prime Minister William Pitt, who resolved to commit the necessary men and equipment to win. The first venture, on 8 July against Fort Carillon, ended in disaster, mainly because of poor judgement on the part of the expedition's commander, Major-General James Abercromby. As though to compensate for this setback, Major-General Jeffrey Amherst, Brigadier James Wolfe, and Admiral Edward Boscawen captured Louisbourg on the 27th. Colonel John Bradstreet captured Fort Frontenac on 25 August, and on 23 November, Brigadier John Forbes forced the French to abandon Fort Duquesne, which he renamed Fort Pitt.

In 1759, the British captured Fort Niagara on 25 July. On the 26th the French withdrew from Carillon, and from Fort St Frédéric on 4 August, but they retained a fleet of warships on Lake Champlain that prevented Amherst from advancing on Montreal. On 13 September, after a summer-long siege, Wolfe defeated Montcalm at Quebec.

By 1760 disaster stared the French in the face, yet Brigadier de Lévis, while attempting to retake Quebec, defeated a British force under Brigadier James Murray on 28 April. Murray retired inside Quebec's walls, and when a British fleet arrived in May, Lévis withdrew to Montreal. Afterwards two final battles were fought. One was a naval engagement at the mouth of the Ristigouche River. On 8 July a British naval squadron under Captain John Byron (grandfather of the poet) defeated a French squadron under Captain François-Gabriel d'Angeac. The last land-water battle the French fought for New France took place in August at the foot of the Thousand Islands in the St. Lawrence River. It was fought between General Amherst's troops and a small body of French regulars and militia on Ile Royale (Chimney Island, New York). Boaters may enjoy tracing the route of the Amherst expedition through the islands and investigating the sites associated with this battle.

Following the Battle of the Thousand Islands, Amherst, who had moved from Oswego, Colonel William Haviland advancing from Lake Champlain, and Brigadier Muray coming from Quebec, converged on Montreal, which capitulated on 8 September 1760. The conquest of New France was complete. There remained only France's attempt to possess Newfoundland in order to obtain concessions from Britain at the peace table.

The war ended with the signing of the Treaty of Paris on 10 February 1763. France lost her entire North American empire, and was left with only her fishing rights in Newfoundland and the islands of St. Pierre and Miquelon. (In addition to Canada and Acadia, France lost Louisiana east of the Mississippi. New Orleans and Louisiana west of the Mississippi had been ceded to Spain in 1762.)

Louisbourg 1745

2

Apart from the Plains of Abraham in Québec, Louisbourg, on Cape Breton Island, is probably Canada's best-known battle field. On-going restoration has made the thirty hectare park a showplace among national historic sites. The story of the largest fortress the French built in Canada began with the signing of the Treaty of Utrecht in 1713. Under its terms France lost Acadia, her claim to Newfoundland, and the Hudson Bay lowland, but she retained New France, Ile Royale (Cape Breton Island) and Ile Saint Jean (Prince Edward Island). Although Ile Saint Jean was raided, no spot can be rightly called a battle ground. However, because the island was administered from Ile Royale, and served as a source of food for the Louisbourg garrison, the battle field at Louisbourg relates to both Prince Edward Island and Cape Breton Island.

France began building Louisbourg in 1719. It was an elaborate community of civilians and soldiers located in a rather unlikely place. The site was close to the Grand Banks fishery, and it was chosen because it could also guard the entrance to New France, but the east coast of Cape Breton, or Ile Royale, was isolated, with a dreary climate and often fogbound. The French officers and troops

View of Louisbourg 1758. In the foreground is Lighthouse Point, where Pepperrell's men erected their gun battery that silenced the Island Battery behind it. The harbour is on the right, and Gabarus Bay is in the background.

Louisbourg 1745

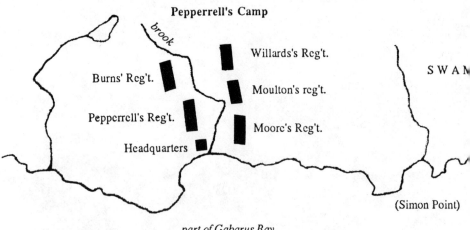

boundary of National Historic Park

Pepperrell's Camp

brook

Burns' Reg't.

Pepperrell's Reg't.

Headquarters

Willards's Reg't.

Moulton's reg't.

Moore's Reg't.

S W A M

(Simon Point)

part of Gabarus Bay

The campaign against Louisbourg showing Pepperrell's position before he advanced beyond the swampy ground. The area now designated a national historic park is outlined.

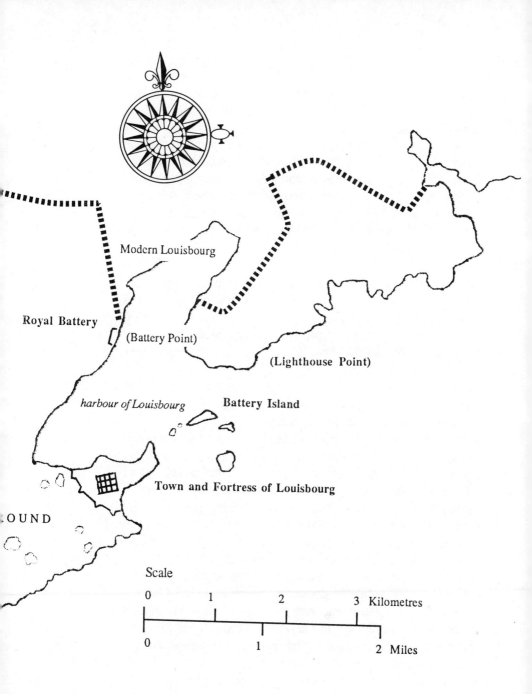

Modern Louisbourg

Royal Battery

(Battery Point)

(Lighthouse Point)

harbour of Louisbourg   **Battery Island**

Town and Fortress of Louisbourg

OUND

Scale

0   1   2   3   Kilometres

0   1   2   Miles

regarded Louisbourg with distaste. Yet for full-time merchants, and officers who indulged in trade on the side, fortunes could be made from the island fortress.

Louisbourg was captured twice. A massive expedition took the fortress in 1758 when success was almost foreordained. That the fortress fell in 1745 was more remarkable. The capture took place during the War of the Austrian Succession (the North American phase was called King George's War). France declared war on Britain on 15 March 1744, and in May, French troops from Louisbourg attacked the closest British settlement, a fishing station at Canso, Nova Scotia. The members of the garrison and others the French found were taken to Louisbourg as prisoners-of-war. From July to October another force from Louisbourg laid siege to Annapolis Royal. The French commander, Lieutenant Joseph Du Vivier, withdrew when a naval reinforcement failed to arrive. But the attack on Annapolis Royal had made the businessmen of New England very apprehensive. New England, and its commerce, would never be secure as long as the French possessed Louisbourg. From prisoners captured at Canso, confined at Louisbourg and exchanged towards the end of the year, the New Englanders learned that the French might well be dislodged from their island fortress.

Two men who were returned to Boston were Joshua Loring and John Bradstreet, and they suggested that Louisbourg was not as formidable as most people had been led to believe. Loring was the captain of a merchant ship that had been captured by the French that summer. Bradstreet was a lieutenant in the Canso garrison. He had been born at Annapolis Royal, of an English father and an Acadian mother. He had been baptised Jean-Baptiste, which he changed to John when he decided to throw in his lot with the English. Both Bradstreet and Loring had noticed many weaknesses in Louisbourg's defences. These were in need of repair, and the garrison was in low spirits. In the garrison were Swiss mercenaries of the Régiment de Karrer as well as French troops, and Bradstreet reported that most of them were in no mood to fight.

Other characters who took an interest in Louisbourg were William Vaughan, wealthy and with a vested interest in the fishery, Commodore Peter Warren of the British fleet that wintered in the West Indies, and William Pepperrell. Warren was from an Anglo-

Irish family and the uncle of Sir William Johnson, later the Superintendent of Indian Affairs. The uncle had married well, for his wife was Susannah DeLancey, of the prestigious New York Huguenot family. Pepperrell was a merchant, a ship owner, and the commander of the Maine militia. (At that time Maine was not a separate colony but a part of Massachusetts). Pepperrell would later be chosen to command the expedition, an amateur leading an army of amateurs. Upon hearing the reports of Joshua Loring and John Bradstreet, the governor of Massachusetts, William Shirley, felt that with some help from the Royal Navy, an army of New Englanders could capture the pride of the French overseas empire.

In January 1745, Shirley placed a request before the Massachusetts General Court that a colonial army of 3,000 volunteers be raised, and a colonial fleet af armed vessels be prepared. On the 5 February the court gave its consent. When informed by Massachusetts, Connecticut and New Hampshire were enthusiastic about the expedition, but Rhode Island was not. New York agreed to provide some cannon but no troops. New Jersey and Quaker Pennsylvania would promise only provisions. Governor Shirley pressed on and he chose William Pepperrell to command the land forces. His subordinates were Brigadier-General Samuel Waldo, who raised his own 2nd Massachusetts Regiment; the Connecticut contingent was led by Major-General Roger Wolcott.

On 4 April, fifty-one transports crammed with 2,800 Massachusetts troops sailed from Boston, escorted by the armed vessels *Shirley* and *Massachusetts*. The sea voyage was a nightmare for many of the volunteers; the waters were rough and the men seasick. The fleet reached Canso on 15 April, to find that troops from New Hampshire had already arrived. Pepperrell had his men erect a blockhouse, for Canso would serve as a forward base for the attack on Louisbourg.

On 3 May, the frigate H.M.S. *Eltham* sailed into view. The following day Commodore Peter Warren's *Superbe*, a 60-gun flagship, arrived escorted by the frigates *Launceston* and *Mermaid*. After conferring with Pepperrell, Warren took his ships off to blockade the entrance to Louisbourg harbour. On the 6th he sent a message to let Pepperrell know that Gabarus Bay was free of ice — information very important to the commander's plans. By the 5th, Pepperrell's other subordinate, Major-General Roger Wolcott, had arrived with 500 men from Connecticut, and the expedition sailed.

Louisbourg was a fortress town on the peninsula overlooking a large harbour with a narrow entrance. The Royal Battery of thirty guns stood on the inner shore of the harbour where the modern town of Louisbourg stands. An island with a battery of thirty-nine guns lay midway across the entrance. These two batteries, and two batteries located in the fortress town, provided effective cross-fire to cover the harbour. To the south of the fortress lay a swampy stretch of land reaching to a rocky shore. The soft ground and inhospitable shore gave the garrison a false sense of security. Louisbourg was not likely to be attacked by land. Gabarus Bay stretched in a long arc west and south of the promontory where the fortress had been built.

Within the walls was a small town where some merchants and civilians lived. The garrison dwelt in barracks inside the walls as did the governor in his palace. In addition, outside the walls of the town and around the harbour were the properties of merchants and fishermen. Settlements of farmers and fishermen were scattered along the east coast of the island.

The garrison consisted of 600 French and Swiss professional troops and some 900 militiamen. In command was the acting governor, sixty-five year old Louis du Pont Duchambon (father of Louis du Pont Duchambon de Vergor, who would be at Beauséjour in 1755 and Quebec in 1759). Duchambon was waiting for a new governor to replace Commandant Jean-Baptiste Louis le Prévost

Early view of Louisbourg. The city changed little in later years, except for the construction of a gateway — The Frédéric — on the quay possibly in 1742.

Model of a 50-gun man-of-war, 1730-1745. This shows a typical man-of-war that sailed between France and New France in the first half of the 18th century.

Duquesnel, the governor, who had died in October 1744. The fortress had ample supplies of food but not of ammunition and powder. Duchambon was aware that Commodore Warren was blockading the harbour, but his ships could not get past the Island Battery. What Duchambon was not prepared for was Pepperrell's choice of a landing site, which was in Garbarus Bay.

Pepperrell's force arrived there on 11 May, a Tuesday. Although the northerly coast of Gabarus Bay was rocky, several coves looped the shore, where boats could be run in to the beaches. Gorham's Rangers, commanded by Shubiel Gorham, would be responsible for transporting the troops to the landing places. That day, thinking that the Royal Battery might be overrun too easily, Duchambon ordered the artillerymen who were manning it spike the thirty guns and come into the main fortress. He made a fateful mistake.

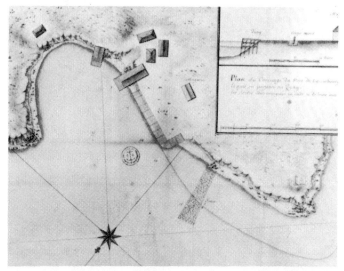

Plan of the drydock at Louisbourg. The signature on the plan is that of the engineer Verrier, and shows the cove in the southeast part of the port. Here sailing vessels were refitted after long voyages.

Restored main building near the King's Bastion, Louisbourg. In this building was the governor's residence, as well as barracks for part of the garrison.

As Pepperrell's men descended into their boats, the surf was running gently. While the men were landing, Duchambon made one half-hearted attempt to discourage Pepperrell. He sent militia officers Pierre Morpain and Antoine Le Poupet de la Boulardière with fifty militia and thirty regulars along the shore. In the lead boat, making for Flat Point Cove, were Captain John Gorham with part of his company of rangers. When Gorham noticed Morpain's men approaching, he gestured, and the boats changed direction, making for a spot three kilometres farther west, where they landed unopposed. Morpain's men came close and fought a brief skirmish before withdrawing back inside Louisbourg. By nightfall, Pepperrell had 2,000 men ashore, and the rest followed on the 12th.

That day, acting on the advice of John Bradstreet, now serving as the lieutenant-colonel of the 1st Massachusetts Regiment, Pepperrell sent William Vaughan with some men to burn and loot warehouses. On their return they informed Pepperrell that the Royal Battery was empty. He sent Brigadier Samuel Waldo with a party

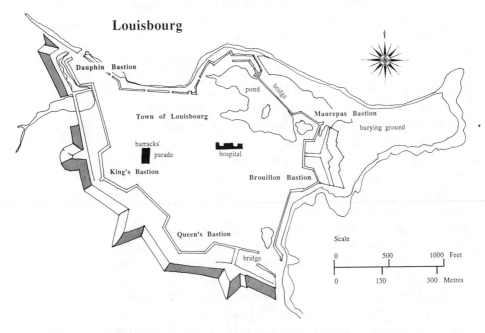

Detailed plan of the defences surrounding the town and fortress of Louisbourg in 1745.

to unspike the thirty guns – a windfall for the new Englanders. Many of the balls which Pepperrell had brought fitted the guns, and Waldo soon had the four embrasures that faced the fortress turned on Louisbourg and firing to deadly effect.

Meanwhile, Pepperrell sent parties out to raid outlying settlements, and set up camp at Simon Point on both sides of a fresh water brook. A contemporary plan showed Willard's, Moulton's and Moore's regiments on the east side of the brook, and Burns' and Pepperrell's regiments on the west side. However only one of these regiments – Pepperrell's – was mentioned in other sources. Pepperrell's own headquarters were at the mouth of the brook on the west side.

Governor Shirley's instructions to Pepperrell had been to try an assault on the fortress, because his untrained volunteers might not be capable of conducting a formal siege. After looking over the ground Pepperrell decided that such a siege was practicable. His men could advance by digging trenches parallel to Louisbourg's walls, linked by zigzag trenches. His army would advance by digging parallel trenches ever closer to the walls, moving the guns to the new trenches so that they could fire with more deadly effect. Then Pepperrell compromised – by having his guns brought forward under cover of darkness and fog, without digging trenches, until they were between the swamp and the walls. Then the men began protecting their guns with barrels filled with earth, and earthworks strengthened with bundles of green sticks called 'fascines'. Duchambon was astonished to discover that the Americans had dragged their guns through the stretch of bog that supposedly protected Louisbourg on the landward side.

Outside, Commodore Warren was growing impatient. He was anxious to penetrate the harbour, which was blocked by the gunners who covered the entrance from the Island Battery. Pepperrell warned Warren that the battery could not be captured without enormous losses. Before he had decided what to do, the French ship *Vigilant*, with sixty-four guns, appeared, bringing ammunition and fifty barrels of powder as well as other supplies for the Louisbourg garrison. A New England privateer spotted the French vessel first, but Warren's ships soon engaged her. *Vigilant* put up a strong fight before surrendering to Warren. The loss of the supply ship bringing sorely needed ammunition further

The Prudent *1758. This ship of 74 guns, one of 12 sent to Louisbourg in 1758, was destroyed by fire at the end of July.*

demoralised the garrison.

Pepperrell made two major attempts to silence the Island Battery. On 2 June, he had Waldo send 800 men in small boats towards the island, but all had to turn back soon after they set out. On the 6th, Waldo sent 400 men in an attempted assault, but they were easily turned back, with losses of 200 killed and wounded and captured, to Warren's exasperation. The two commanders were friends, and they worked well together, but both were edgy at the awesome undertaking at hand, and beginning to wonder if they could succeed. Numbers were on their side, but many of the men were ill, and both commanders knew that a small force behind strong walls might well be a match for them.

Pepperrell reported to Warren that his men had erected five fascine batteries with sixteen guns and mounted mortars. The cannon from the Royal Battery had been firing on the town, to the distress of the inhabitants, and the wall had been breached in several places, especially at the west gate which was partly demolished. He described his efforts to reduce the Island Battery and explained why he had failed thus far. His men were fatigued because so much work had to be done, and so many had fallen ill that he had only 2,100 effectives.

Warren had his own troubles. He was operating in dangerous waters, plagued by frequent fogs. Fortuitously, by 21 June, Pepperrell reported that he solved his problem over how to deal with the Island Battery. His men were erecting a gun battery on Lighthouse Point, at the north side of the harbour entrance. Once the guns began firing, the position of the gunners in the Island Battery became untenable and they withdrew. That day, hoping to intimidate the French, Warren sent an officer with a flag of truce to invite Duchambon to surrender to the navy. The professional naval officers would treat the French more kindly than would the irregulars from New England. About that time some vessels arrived from England to join Warren, bringing his strength to six ships-of-the-line and five frigates, with a total of 554 guns and 3,585 officers, seamen and marines.

By 26 June, Pepperrell and Warren were ready for a final assault should there be no surrender. Louisbourg had been hit by 9,000 cannon balls and 600 exploding shells. One report stated that only three houses were habitable, another that only one house remained standing. With his ammunition nearly exhausted, the fortress a shambles, Duchambon sent messages to Pepperrell and Warren asking for terms. On the 27th, during negotiations, the two commanders promised that property would be respected – a condition bound to frustrate many of the volunteer New Englanders who had enlisted mainly for the opportunity to plunder. Duchambon agreed that the formal surrender would take place on the 28th.

Warren made certain that a detachment of his marines was the first to reach the fortress. Because of his move, and his earlier suggestion that the French surrender to the navy, Warren has been accused of stealing Pepperrell's thunder. All Warren sought was an orderly transfer of power, one that might not occur if the New Englanders were the first to enter Louisbourg. Once they saw that they could not plunder, many of the New Englanders became disenchanted with the expedition and only wanted to get back home.

If they could not steal from the people of Louisbourg, there remained Ile Saint Jean, which belonged to the fortress. On 20 June, a party of New Englanders raided the future Prince Edward Island and destroyed the settlement of Acadians at Port-La-Joye (Charlottetown).

When the news of the capture of Louisbourg reached England,

Pepperrell was awarded a baronetcy, and Warren was promoted to rear admiral. Warren was less pleased to discover that he had been appointed the first British governor of Cape Breton Island. The French troops and civilians were sent to Rochfort, France, and jubilation resounded throughout New England. Pepperrell's army of amateurs had triumphed. The news struck France like a thunderbolt. How could a fortress built and maintained at such enormous expense have fallen so easily?

Louisbourg had to be retaken. In 1746 a large fleet carrying French troops left the mother country to rendez-vous with a force of militia and *troupes de la marine* moving from Quebec. After being battered by Atlantic storms, the soldiers and sailors stricken with illness, the French fleet took refuge in Chebucto Bay (Halifax harbour) and from there it returned to France. The force from Quebec raided Grand Pré and went back home.

To the fury of the New England people, the French were able to reoccupy Louisbourg just three years later, in 1748. During the bargaining that led to the Treaty of Aix-la-Chapelle that ended the War of the Austrian Succession, Britain agreed to return Louisbourg to France.

In 1758, during the Seven Years' War (or French and Indian War), a combined naval and military force again captured Louisbourg. The battle was on a much larger scale, but the approach was much the same. The land force was commanded by Major-General Jeffrey Amherst, whose army amounted to 13,000 men. The naval force, under the command of Admiral Edward Boscawen, consisted of 14,000 sailors and marines. The fleet of 157 vessels mounted 1,842 guns. The attack began on 28 May 1758. An early move was the occupation of the site of the Royal Battery (it had been demolished in 1757), and again guns from that spot were turned on Louisbourg. For a second time, artillery placed on Lighthouse Point bombarded the Island Battery, this time under the direction of Brigadier James Wolfe, the victor at Quebec the following year. Louisbourg was defended by four regiments of French regulars, twenty-four companies of *troupes de la marine* and 4,000 sailors and militia under the governor, Augustin Boschenry de Drucour. With the Island Battery out of action, the British fleet was in a position to gain again the harbour. The garrison surrendered, on 26 July, after almost two months.

On 8 August, Amherst dispatched a force to Ile Saint Jean. The troops built Fort Amherst at Port-La-Joye to secure the island. Some 300 Acadians in remote areas managed to stay out of sight, but 3,500 were deported to France. Afterwards Prince Edward Island was surveyed and township-sized parcels were granted to proprietors in Britain and Canada.

In 1760 the British garrison systematically demolished the fortress of Louisbourg to ensure that the French could not make use of it again without going to enormous expense. The site was abandoned, and since it was not suitable for other uses, it remained for the most part deserted. The present town of Louisbourg grew on the west side of the harbour where the Royal Battery stood, a more sheltered spot than the promintory. The place where the fortress had been built was available for a national historic park where, from old French records and archaeological evidence, a magnificent restoration has taken place.

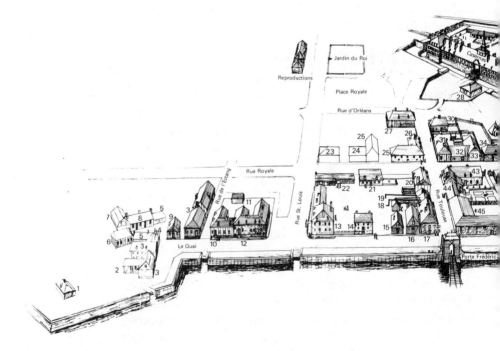

Map of restored Louisbourg. A comparison with earlier plans shows how much of the original structure has not been rebuilt.

1 Corps de garde/Guardhouse
2 Magasin Baron
3 Magasin Delort
4 Maison Chevalier
5 Magasin Cassagnolles-Detcheverry
6 Maison Baron
7 Magasin Santier
8 Maison Santier
9 Maison Morin
10 Maison de Cressonet dit Beauséjour
11 Magasin La Grange
12 Maison La Grange
13 Résidence du Commissaire Ordonnateur/
   Financial Commissary's Residence
14 Maison de Pugnant dit Destouches
15 Auberge d'Auger dit Grandchamp
16 Maison d'Auger dit Grandchamp
17 Hôtel de la Marine
18 Auberge de l'Epée Royale

19 Maison Benoist
20 Maison Carrerot
21 Maison Dugas
22 Etables du Commissaire Ordonnateur/
   Financial Commissary's Stables
23 Maison Fizel
24 Maison Loppinot
25 Magasin De La Vallière
26 Maison De La Vallière
27 Maison De La Plagne
28 Corps de garde/Guardhouse
29 Galerie de mines/Mine Gallery
30 Maison De Gannes de Falaise
31 Maison Rodrigue
32 Magasin Rodrigue
33 Magasin De La Pérelle
34 Maison De La Pérelle
35 Glacière/Icehouse
36 Maison Duhaget

37 Cour à bois de la garnison/
   Garrison Woodlot
38 Boulangerie/Bakery
39 Forge d'artillerie/Artillery Forge
40 Forge d'armurerie/Armoury Forge
41 Hangard/Storehouse
42 Buanderie/Laundry
43 Résidence de l'Ingénieur/
   Engineer's Residence
44 Ancien Magasin/Old Storehouse
45 Magasin du Roi/King's Storehouse
46 Hangard d'artillerie/Artillery Storehouse
47 Four à chaux/Lime Kiln
48 Maison Lartigue
49 Courtine/Curtain Wall
50 Poterne/Postern
51 Casernes/Barracks
52 Poudrière/Powder Magazine
53 Corps de garde/Guardrooms
54 Eperon

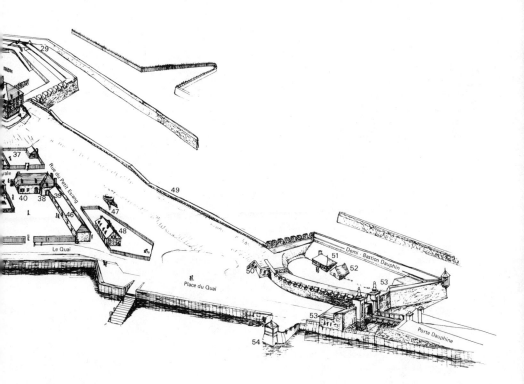

Fort Beauséjour 1755

3

The main event of King George's War 1744-1748 (in Europe the War of Austrian Succession) was the capture of Louisbourg. Under the terms of the Treaty of Aix la Chapelle that ended the war, Louisbourg was returned to France, and Britain's ownership of the peninsula of Acadia (Nova Scotia) was confirmed. In 1749 Britain started building her great naval base at Halifax and began bringing in settlers. France hoped that the part of Acadia which is now New Brunswick would be retained as French territory.

To limit British expansion and to hold the land north of the Bay of Fundy as well as protect the remaining Acadian settlements, France began building Fort Beauséjour in 1751. The fort was pentagon-shaped, with five bastions. These, the casements in the curtain wall, and the other buildings, were of timber. The main structure was reinforced with a ditch and elevated slope, or glacis. It was strategically placed on the west side of the Missaguash River, overlooking the Bay of Fundy and the Tantramar Marshes, part of which had already been drained because in establishing farms, the Acadians preferred draining marshland to clearing forests. At the other end of the Isthmus of Chignecto, the French built Fort Gaspereau as a supply base to Beauséjour. Gaspereau stood on the

Contemporary view of Fort Beauséjour. The fort was on high ground overlooking the marshes, but over-looked by a ridge extending inland.

Beauséjour

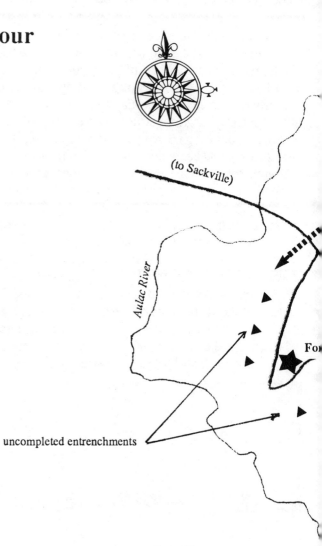

(to Sackville)

Aulac River

Fo...

uncompleted entrenchments

Bay of Fundy

Scale

0   1   2   3 Kilometres

0   1   2 Miles

The siege of Fort Beauséjour 1755

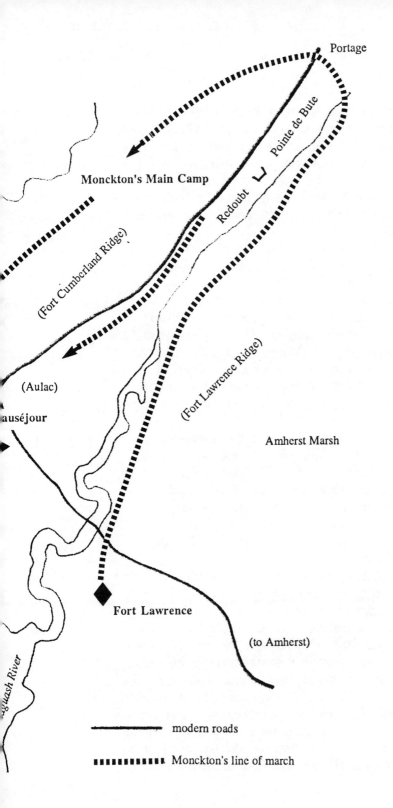

Portage

Pointe de Bute

Monckton's Main Camp

Redoubt

(Fort Cumberland Ridge)

(Fort Lawrence Ridge)

(Aulac)

auséjour

Amherst Marsh

Fort Lawrence

(to Amherst)

...quash River

———————— modern roads

▪▪▪▪▪▪▪▪▪▪▪ Monckton's line of march

49

shore of Baie Verte (near the site of Port Elgin). It lay on the more direct route linking the French posts in Acadia with Ile Saint Jean (Prince Edward Island) , Louisbourg, and Quebec – the latter two, the source of garrisons and supplies.

To reinforce her ownership, France encouraged her former Acadian subjects to move from the lands under British control and resettle around Beauséjour. Some did come from Beaubassin, Nappan, and Macan.

Many other Acadians preferred to remain in their original settlements but refused to take an unconditional oath of allegiance to Britain. They really wanted to remain neutral and to avoid being disloyal to either power.

Before the French started Fort Beauséjour, the British had built Fort Lawrence on the south side of the Missaguash River, and a scant three kilometres away. The Missaguash became an unofficial boundary between the disputed territory occupied by the French and British Nova Scotia. The British fort was named for Charles Lawrence, the lieutenant governor who by 1755 had succeeded the first governor, Edward Cornwallis.

Residing at Fort Beauséjour in 1755 were the commandant, Jean-Baptiste Mutigny de Vassan and a few colonial regulars, most ot them *troupes de la marine*. Also on hand was the soldier-priest of the Spiritan order, the Abbé Jean Le Loutre. He was notorious among the British settlers for inciting his Micmac converts to attack their homes.

In command at Fort Lawrence in 1752 and 1753 was the man who would lead the expedition against Beauséjour in 1755 – Lieutenant-Colonel Robert Monckton, then of the 47th Regiment of Foot. He maintained communications with Beauséjour, for the records show he exchanged notes, deserters and runaway horses with Beauséjour's commandant, Vassan. In 1753, he moved to Halifax , and early in 1755, when hostilities between France and Britain were increasing, he was in Boston planning his expedition.

Matters were coming to a head between Britain and France. The main issue was the ownership of the Ohio Valley. British colonists wanted room to expand. France wanted to keep open a line of communication to the Mississippi and Louisiana. Protecting the route was Fort Duquesne (the site of Pittsburgh, Pennsylvania) . In the spring, a large expedition led by Major-General Edward Braddock had been sent against the fort .

Assisting Monckton in Boston was the governor of Massachusetts, William Shirley. From New England, Monckton would take two battalions of provincial troops, some 2,000 men, commanded by Lieutenant-Colonels John Winslow and George Scott. Monckton planned to rendez-vous in the Annapolis Basin with some British regulars, many of them artillerymen, from Halifax. The number of regulars on the expedition was 270, but some were from the Fort Lawrence garrison.

Fort Beauséjour & Fort Lawrence
(Based on PAC Map Collection H4/205 not to scale)

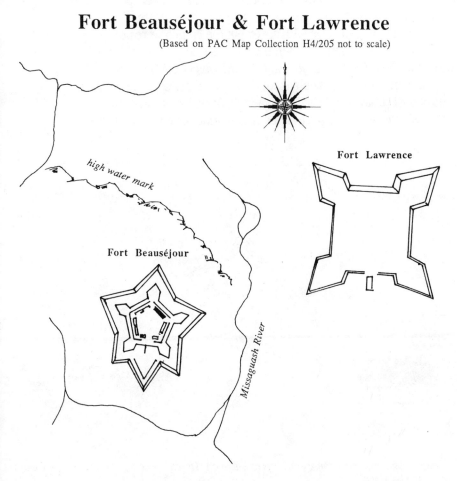

Contrasting designs of Beauséjour and Lawrence. Based on a contemporary map, the drawings are not in scale, nor are the distances between the two forts accurate.

In the thirty-one vessel flotilla that sailed from Boston were the twenty-gun frigate *Success* with Lieutenant-Colonel Winslow aboard, the schooner *Lawrence* carrying Lieutenant-Colonel Monckton, two other frigates, some snows, sloops, brigantines and schooners. This fleet arrived off Annapolis on 25 May. Within five days it had been joined by the sloop *Vulture* and six small troop transports bringing the regulars from Halifax. The combined fleet sailed on 1 June and lay near the mouth of the Missaguash River the following day. At about 6.00 p.m. Monckton began landing troops and two 6-pounder cannon on the east side of the river. The troops marched to Fort Lawrence, which would serve as a base and as cover. Monckton had acted with speed but the French were not taken by surprise for they had seen the fleet as it approached.

The commandant of Beauséjour at the time was Louis Du Pont Duchambon de Vergor, an unpleasant debauched character, and a friend of the equally debauched Intendant Bigot. Vergor's garrison was 175 colonial regulars from *troupes de la marine*, Le Loutre and

Contemporary diagram of Fort Beauséjour with cross-section. The cross-section shows the log and earth structure of the bastions.

his Micmac followers, and such Acadians as could be coerced into serving. About 1,200 to 1,500 Acadians lived in the neighbourhood, and Vergor embodied 300 of them from his militia. Vergor was an incompetent soldier, but he had courage, and he did manage to have his men destroy a bridge – Pont à Bout – over the Missaguash, and to break dikes and flood some land to impede the progress of Monckton's force.

Some of Vergor's garrison were in a redoubt near Point de Bute close to the destroyed bridge, and there the first encounter took place, apart from a little skirmishing by scouts and Indians. The French in the redoubt opened fire with cannon and muskets. Monckton's two 6-pounders replied. After a quarter of an hour the French set fire to the redoubt and to some houses, to prevent the British using them as cover, and withdrew into Fort Beauséjour.

For the next few days little happened other than lively skirmishing. A British sergeant and ten privates were killed, while the French lost three soldiers and one Indian killed. In the meantime Monckton and his officers were reconnoitering the locality. The logical approach was from the northeast. A ridge ran inland from Beauséjour that was roughly parallel to the Missaguash River. By placing guns there, Monckton could get them within range to pound the fort. He decided to move two more guns to that position, and to march his men up the east side of the Missaguash, crossing over well above Beauséjour, and attaining the ridge in the vicinity of Aulac. From there he could move his guns forward. Most of the troops would be used to encircle the fort, and the men would dig siege trenches for protection. All this took time, because the French fired on his positions, which meant entrenchments at every advance. His guns were not ready to begin firing on the fort until 13 June, by which time he had not encircled Beauséjour completely.

The firing had a demoralizing effect on the garrison inside Beauséjour. On the 16th, before Monckton was ready to begin the siege in earnest, – his entrenchments still incomplete – Vergor sent him an offer of surrender. Abbé Le Loutre, fearful of capture after the activities of his Micmacs, slipped away, through the woods to set out for Quebec. Monckton agreed to allow the Beauséjour garrison passage to Louisbourg and he pardoned the Acadian irregulars who had been pressed into service by Vergor, pending instructions from Halifax. By that time Lieutenant-Colonel

Beauséjour is being restored and is a national historic park. The excavation work was in process in 1966 when this photograph was taken.

Winslow, at the head of part of his battalion, was marching for Fort Gaspereau. On the 17th or 18th, Benjamin Rouer de Villeray, the commandant of Fort Gaspereau, accepted the same terms as Vergor, and did not offer Winslow any resistance.

Monckton had accomplished his task in less time and with fewer losses than he had anticipated. With the manpower at his disposal, he began repairing and enlarging Fort Beauséjour , now renamed Fort Cumberland in honour of the commander-in-chief of the British army. Monckton soon received a distasteful order from Governor Charles Lawrence. Some representatives of the Acadian people had been meeting with Lawrence in Halifax, and as they had always done, refused to take the unconditional oath of allegiance. Lawrence decided that the time had come to use military power to expel the Acadians. He ordered Monckton to carry out the expulsion in the Chignecto area, to punish them for taking up arms; they were not permitted the opportunity to take the oath of

Model of Fort Beauséjour showing the entire structure that is on display at the restored fort.

Artist's rendition of the dismantling of Fort Beauséjour by the French.

Artist's interpretation of the French surrendering the fort to the British.

allegiance. Although he disapproved, Monckton set about the task efficiently, arresting Acadians, sending sodiers to burn their villages, and supervising the deportation of about 1,100 unfortunates.

Abbé Le Loutre, who had been one of the causes of trouble for the British in Nova Scotia, succeeded in reaching Quebec. On 15 September he sailed for France. His ship was captured by a British squadron and he was held prisoner for eight years. Not until the peace treaty was signed in 1763 was he released.

Beauséjour was the only British success of 1755, the year before the Seven Years' War officially began. Braddock's attempt to capture Fort Duquesne ended in disaster and his death. Monckton continued serving efficiently. As the colonel-commandant of the 2nd battalion, 60th Royal American Regiment, he later stood on the Plains of Abraham as James Wolfe's senior brigadier-general.

Fort Carillon (Ticonderoga) 1758

4

The French began building Fort Carillon in 1755, under the direction of Michel Chartier, later the Marquis de Lotbinière. He selected the site, overlooking Lake Champlain where Wood Creek enters it. This battle ground is in New York State, on the west side of Lake Champlain, near the present town of Ticonderoga, New York. Although not in Canada, the Ticonderoga promontory where Fort Carillon was built, was the scene of considerable action of the utmost importance to Canada, at first in the hostilities between the British and French in North America, and later between the British and the American rebels. Carillon was the advance post protecting New France as was Fort St Frédéric, at Crown Point, an earlier fortification guarding the Hudson-Champlain-Richlieu gateway. In the spring of 1758, Major-General James Abercromby, the commander-in-chief of British forces in North America, led a massive attack on Carillon.

Of Abercromby, the late Charles H.J. Snider remarked that the

Modern view of the restored Fort Ticonderoga, originally Fort Carillon. The fort stands on a promontory on the west side of Lake Champlain.

Strategic Postion of Fort Carillon

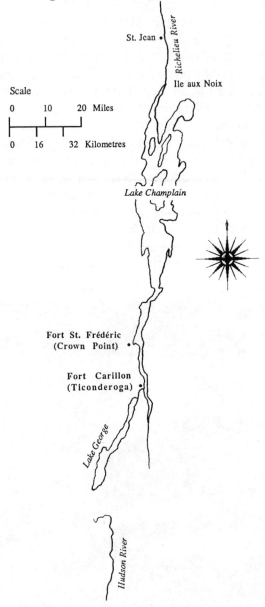

Fort Carillon (now Ticonderoga) was placed on a promontory where Lake Champlain narrows and at the base of the outlet from Lake George. Behind the fort, on both sides, rise mountains that were a barrier difficult to bypass.

only clever thing he ever did was to send his quartermaster, John Bradstreet, to capture Fort Frontenac. Allan Maclean, a lieutenant in the 4th battalion of the 60th Regiment, would have argued with Snider. Maclean had cause to be grateful to Abercromby for ridding him of a hated, brutal Swiss battalion commander, Colonel James Prevost. In defiance of the Duke of Cumberland, the commander of all the King's forces who made Prevost something of a protegé, Abercromby relieved the Swiss of his command. Abercromby was a tireless worker and a useful staff officer, but his capacities as a field commander were severely limited.

Abercromby's force amounted to some 15,000 men – 7,000 of them British regulars from seven regiments – the 1st or Royal Regiment of Foot, the 27th, 34th, 42nd, 44th, 46th, and part of the 1st battalion and all of the 4th battalion of the 60th Regiment. The first six named were brought from Britain, but the 60th was raised in the colonies and named the Royal American Regiment. Abercromby also had some 8,000 provincial troops, which included ranger companies under the overall command of Major Robert Rogers, famous for his men's abilities in conducting guerrilla warfare.

The vast expedition gathered at Albany, on the upper Hudson River. There John Bradstreet had superintended the construction of hundreds of bateaux to carry troops and supplies as far as the great bend in the Hudson, where some sixteen kilometres of land separated the river from Lake George. At the foot of that lake, Bradstreet had troops constructing bateaux and whaleboats for the transport of men and supplies, and rafts for carrying artillery

Fort St. Frédéric (Crown Point) in 1759, a contemporary sketch. Like Carillon, the fort at Crown Point was abandoned in 1759 because the garrison was needed to reinforce Montreal.

pieces. An army of 15,000 men was not large by modern standards, but moving it and supplying it in nearly uninhabited country with few roads was an almost overwhelming task involving backbreaking toil.

Abercromby's second-in-command was the popular Brigadier-General George Augustus, Viscount Howe, who was also the colonel of the 55th Regiment, but who, after the campaign, was to transfer to the 3rd battalion of the 60th Regiment.

While the British force was preparing to move north, the French inside Carillon were stenghtening their defences. They were erecting a long line of log and earth walls and small redoubts to stretch from one side of the promontory to the other, some 900 metres west and north of the main fort. At the southern end, this chain of advance posts was protected by a bluff and a wall. The northeastern end was the vulnerable one, as the ground sloped gently down to Lake Champlain. The promontory is at the spot where Lake George empties eastwards down Rivière des Chutes. The rapids in this stream are shallow and did not form a barrier for bateaux. In front of their chain of outposts the French placed abatis – small felled trees and large branches – placed with their trunks and limbs against the log and earth walls so that an attacker had to struggle through a tangle of branches, often with points sharpened, before reaching the breastworks.

At Carillon, as Abercromby approached, was the French commander-in-chief, Field Marshall the Marquis de Montcalm. His subordinates were Brigadier-General the Chevalier de Lévis and Colonel Charles de Bourlamaque. Montcalm's garrison was described as 3,600 men – eight battalions of regulars, the regiments La Sarre, Languedoc, Béarn, Guyenne, Royal Rousillon, La Reine, and the 1st and 2nd Bérry. French numerical strength was inferior, but Montcalm held the fortified positions. Abercromby's task was to break through Carillon's defences, if he could.

By mid-June, Abercromby's entire force was at Fort Edward, at the top of the bend in the Hudson River, and was starting the journey overland to Lake George. Officers and ranks alike marched, for all the horses were needed to haul the supply wagons. By 4 July, the whole force had reached the site of Fort William Henry, at the foot of Lake George, which Montcalm had captured and destroyed in August 1757. There Abercromby's army embarked in 800 bateaux and 90 whaleboats, the artillery pieces riding on the wooden rafts. The long flotilla made a stirring sight. Flags were flying, fifes and drums and the pipes of the Highlanders playing frequently. The green coats of the rangers contrasted with the scarlet of the regulars. On either side of Lake George rose forested mountains.

The army disembarked on 6 July in a cove at the head of the lake and set up a base camp. All the women and servants would remain there, and Abercromby's advance force, under Brigadier Howe, prepared to move on Carillon at once. Howe's command included the light companies from all the regular regiments, and these were under direct command of Lieutenant-Colonel Frederick Haldimand, a future governor of Canada. The rest of the regulars were forming

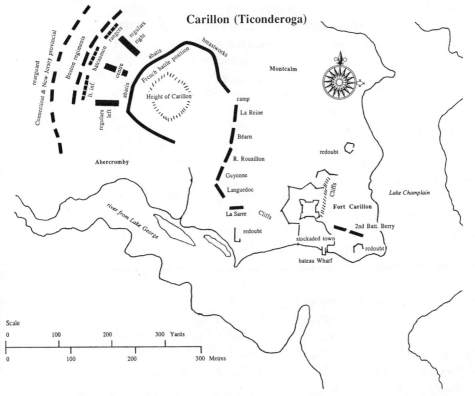

Battle plan at Fort Carillon, 8 July 1758. Abercromby's attacking forces are shown drawn up on the left. Montcalm moved his regulars from their camp outside Carillon to positions behind breastworks and abatis.

three columns to follow after Howe. Rangers would operate on the left flank and the light companies on the right.

While the British force was deploying, Montcalm brought his eight battalions of regulars to his forward positions, surrounding a height of land. His left wing, commanded by Bourlamaque, was made up of the regiments La Reine, Guyenne and Béarn, who guarded the portage over Rivière des Chutes. Montcalm commanded the centre, of the La Sarre, Royal Rousillon, Languedoc and 1st Bérry regiments. The 2nd Bérry remained close to the main fort, positioned east of it. At that time the Chevalier de Lévis was scouting with some picked men.

Howe's advance force was marching by a roundabout way, along the left bank of Rivière des Chutes, to avoid having to portage that waterway, and was approaching Trout Brook when it ran into a French force that had become lost while trying to return to Carillon. The ensuing fight was a confusing one, and some of the British troops fired on their own side. Six French officers and 150 other ranks were killed or taken prisoner. When this small battle ended, the troops found that their favourite commander, Howe, was among the dead, a result that had a very demoralizing effect on the British army.

On 7 July, Abercromby changed his mind about the route of march and decided on a more direct approach to Carillon. Instead of using the circuitous route along Rivière des Chutes, he had his entire force ford the stream. That morning, Sir William Johnson, the Superintendent of Indian Affairs, arrived from the Mohawk Valley at the head of a large party of Iroquois warriors. They took up a position high on Sugar Hill that overlooked the fort, but their musket fire did not disturb Montcalm's troops. While the regulars forded the stream, the rangers provided a screen to deal with any French pickets in the area. The army camped near the shore that night, ready to attack the next day, the 8th.

At dawn the army rose, and the regulars, in three columns, formed the advance force. The light companies, bateau crews and rangers formed an extended line behind the columns, with a rear guard of provincials from Boston, Connecticut and New Jersey. Now the stage was set for a British disaster. On the advice of some of his engineers, Abercromby decided that an artillery bombardment would not be necessary. Instead of softening up the enemy with plenty of heavy artillery fire, Abercromby ordered a frontal assault immediately.

Montcalm had formed up his forward line ready for the arrival of the British columns. At dawn the French troops took up their positions at the forward line of defence along the log and earth wall. Holding the left were the La Sarre and Languedoc regiments with pickets of Canadians and some volunteers, all commanded by Bourlamaque. Montcalm was with the centre, of the 1st Bérry and the Royal Rousillon regiments. The strongest portion was on the right, where the gentle slope down to the water was the easiest to penetrate. There the Chevalier de Lévis commanded the La Reine, Béarn, and Guyenne Regiments, and some colonial troops. Behind each of these three divisions stood a company of grenadiers and a picket as reserves.

Montcalm must have been surprised and overjoyed when no artillery began firing on his defences. Instead, the columns of highly-trained, steady regulars moved purposefully towards his abatis. Those in front were soon floundering against the branches while the French gunners poured down a merciless hail of grape and cannister shot. The soldiers soon disappeared under clouds of blue smoke, and when it cleared the regulars tried again, those farther back crowding forward against those in the front bearing the brunt of the French artillery and musket fire. By mid-afternoon the regulars were still trying to attain the outer chain of defences, and the number of casualties was reaching an appalling level. At length, Abercromby gave the order to the drummers to beat the retreat.

The British had lost some 1,600 fine troops. Lieutenant-Colonel Frederick Haldimand and Lieutenant Allan Maclean were among those wounded. At the same time, Abercromby still had 5,000 able-bodied regulars, and his provincials had hardly been engaged. He might have brought up his artillery and after a proper bombardment tried another assault, but he did not. He had lost his nerve. In failing to capture Carillon he lost further opportunities to command an army in the field. When word of the debacle reached London, he was recalled. The man who replaced him was Jeffrey Amherst, who had captured Louisbourg on 26 July. The other British success of the 1758 campaign season was John Bradstreet's capture of Fort Frontenac (Kingston) on 27 August.

Chevalier de Lévis, later the Duc de Lévis, who was Montcalm's second-in-command at Carillon. After Montcalm's death at Quebec, the chevalier succeeded him as commander-in-chief.

Fort Carillon remained in French hands until July 1759, when Montcalm ordered it abandoned because he did not have enough troops to hold it. At that time he was coping with the British army under General James Wolfe, who had not yet found the right route to breach the defences of Quebec. Soon after the French withdrew, the British occupied Carillon and renamed it Fort Ticonderoga. In May 1775, before the American Revolution officially began, some rebels led by Benedict Arnold and Ethan Allen captured Ticonderoga from its small caretaker garrison. Then in July 1777, General John Burgoyne's troops retook the fort easily, hauling two guns to the top of Sugar Hill and erecting a battery. The gunners renamed the hill Mount Defiance, a name still used, and opened fire on Ticonderoga. The American rebel garrison waited until dark

Painting by Harry A. Ogden of Montcalm congratulating his victorious troops after the battle of 8 July 1758.

and evacuated the fort. A British garrison occupied it until after Burgoyne surrendered his army at Saratoga that October. The garrison then abandoned the fort and retired inside Canada. Afterwards the structure was allowed to fall into ruin. Settlers nearby removed many of the stones to use in building their houses. In 1820, the New York businessman, William Ferris Pell, purchased the deeds to Ticonderoga and the old garrison grounds. The Pell family, generation by generation, has rebuilt the fort, an unusual restoration because it has been done privately instead of with the assistance of government agencies.

A number of other historic battlefields that are relevant to Canadian history are outside the country. One is Fort Niagara, New York, opposite Niagara-on-the-Lake. North of the fort, on the river road, at a spot called La Belle Famille, French reinforcements coming from Presqu'ile (Erie, Pennsylvania) were ambushed and dispersed by a force under Sir William Johnson. The fort surrendered to Johnson on 25 July 1759, the day after the ambush.

Monument to General Montcalm at Fort Ticonderoga. The monument stands in the park close to the road approach to the restored fort.

Another place of interest is Fort Michilimackinac, on Mackinac Island, Michigan. The fort was built by the British in 1780, during the American Revolution, to replace a French fort on the mainland that was set low and easy to attack. Like Carillon, Beauséjour and Frontenac, the French Fort Michilimackinac could be fired upon from a nearby height. In failing to fortify a height of land, the French lost Beauséjour and Frontenac, and the American rebels of 1777 lost Ticonderoga.

The British fleet on Lake Ontario in 1757. Both sides maintained fleets on the inland lakes during the Seven Years' War. Vessels were often captured, refitted and renamed. Some ships were renamed to make the enemy think that the fleet was larger than it was.

Quebec 1759

5

On this most famous of Canadian historic sites what has been called the most decisive battle in Canadian history was fought. The names Wolfe and Montcalm have become deeply engraved on the national consciousness — the two leaders slain, the first following his greatest achievement, the second midst his saddest hour. Here France lost Canada; what followed was the denouement. Because part of the site is now parkland, the battle is fairly easy to envisage. In 1759 thick woods ringed the open plain named for Abraham Martin.

The site of Quebec was chosen in 1608 by Champlain for its defensive potential, and in truth the fortress was so well sited that it came close to foiling Wolfe. Perched high on the cliff, the stronghold was isolated by the St. Lawrence and St. Charles Rivers. Only on its landward quarter was it vulnerable, for the stone wall protecting it was not an impregnable barrier.

The commander-in-chief in New France was Field-Marshall Louis-Joseph de Montcalm-Gagzon, Marquis de Montcalm, Sieur de St. Véran, a small, neat man, forty-seven and a career soldier. His professional subordinates were the forty-year-old Brigadier-General François (or Gaston-François) the Chevalier de Lévis who commanded at Montreal, and Colonel Louis Antoine de Bougainville, at twenty-seven a distinguished scientist and a member of the Royal Society of Great Britain. The other character of note was Canadian-born Pierre de Riguad de Vaudreuil, Marquis de Vaudreuil-Cavagnal, age sixty, who disapproved of imported French officers. Vaudreuil had been at odds with Montcalm since the latter's arrival in 1756 at the beginning of the war.

Montcalm's force at Quebec amounted to five battalions of French regular troops — the Regiments of La Sarre, Languedoc, Béarn, Guyenne and Royal Rousillon — and from 5,000 to 6,000 militiamen, the latter commanded by Vaudreuil, and 2,760 *troupes de la marine*. Montcalm had fortified the area known as the Beauport shore, between the St. Charles and Montmorency Rivers, a stretch where an enemy could penetrate easily. To the west, Montcalm had stationed Bougainville with some 2,000 men, to keep open communication to Montreal and to protect his lines of supply inland.

The grenadier companies of the five regular regiments, a few regulars from the battalion companies, some Canadians, 200

The Quebec Campaign 1759

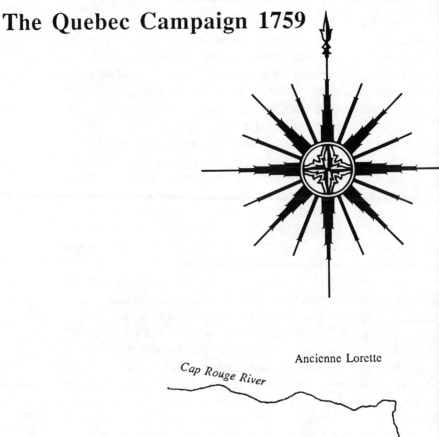

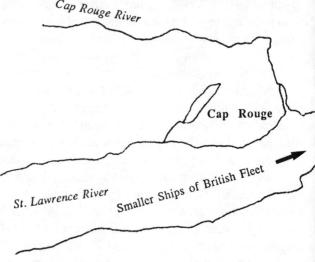

Ancienne Lorette

Cap Rouge River

Cap Rouge

St. Lawrence River

Smaller Ships of British Fleet

In the early stages Wolfe's campaign was against the Beauport shore east of Quebec City. He succeeded when he managed to penetrate the defences of the stronghold from the west and the path up l'Anse au Foulon.

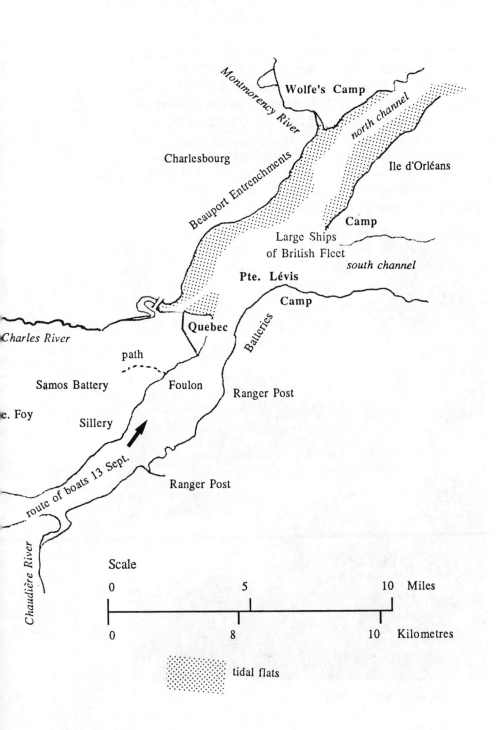

Wolfe's Camp

Montmorency River

Charlesbourg

Beauport Entrenchments

north channel

Ile d'Orléans

Camp

Large Ships
of British Fleet

south channel

Pte. Lévis

Camp

Quebec

Batteries

Charles River

path

Samos Battery

Foulon

Ranger Post

e. Foy

Sillery

route of boats 13 Sept.

Ranger Post

Chaudière River

Scale

0	5	10 Miles

0	8	10 Kilometres

tidal flats

71

cavalry, and 400 to 500 Indians — about 1,000 men — formed Bougainville's most mobile unit. Preventing the British landing upriver from Quebec was of utmost importance to Montcalm. Twenty ships loaded with supplies had arrived from France before the British fleet arrived to blockade the St. Lawrence. Montcalm had sent this fleet upstream to Batiscan, 100 kilometres away, where it would be safe from attack.

Major-General James Wolfe was anything but small and neat. He streched six feet, three inches into the air, scrawny and gangling. The red-headed Wolfe was thirty-five. His subordinates were three brigadier-generals, in order of seniority Robert Monckton (the victor

View of Quebec during the siege of 1759.

of Beauséjour in 1755), George Townshend and James Murray. Every bit as remarkable as Wolfe was the naval commander of the expedition, Vice-Admiral Charles Saunders, who would be responsible for the very tricky operation of landing an army in a tidal zone after charting a treacherous part of the St. Lawrence. Saunders' subordinates were Rear-Admirals Charles Holmes and Philip Durell, the latter of the Halifax naval squadron.

The British expedition was to form up at Louisbourg, but when Saunders and Holmes arrived from England with a fleet on 30 April, they found the ice impassable and moved on to Halifax. Durell had hoped to depart to blockade the St. Lawrence weeks sooner, but a severe winter had kept him in port. He left on 5 May with twenty-seven warships, more than half Saunder's battle fleet. All told, the fleet consisted of forty-nine warships, twenty-two of them ships of the line, each carrying fifty or more guns. The warships remaining with Saunders would move on to Louisbourg and escort 119 transport vessels, carrying supplies and troops. The forty-nine warships were manned by 13,500 sailors of the Royal Navy, the transports by 5,000 merchant seamen. Most of the transports carried flat-bottomed boats for amphibious operations.

Wolfe's army gathered at Louisbourg, awaiting the arrival of the fleet. It consisted of ten regiments of foot, the grenadier companies of three regiments of foot that would remain behind and known as the Louisbourg Grenadiers, three companies of artillerymen, and six companies of Major Robert Rogers' American rangers. This 8,500 man army of regulars was organized in three divisions, each under a brigadier. The quartermaster-general was Colonel Guy Carleton, a future governor of Canada.

When the fleet from Louisbourg arrived in the lower St. Lawrence, it was joined by Durell, whose fleet had been preparing a safe channel. The master aboard the ship *Pembroke*, James Cook, had been setting out buoys and gaining experience as a navigator. By 26 June the fleet was off the Ile d'Orléans, and Wolfe had selected three spots for encampments. The first detachments landed on the Ile d'Orléans on the 26th. The following night Montcalm sent seven fire ships towards the British fleet, but sailors in small rowboats towed them away and prevented any damage to the ships. Wolfe's second detachment occupied Pointe Lévis and built a gun battery to bombard Quebec. Wolfe set up his headquarters on the third site, the east side of the Montmorency River. There he wrestled with the problem of how to break Montcalm's defences. On 1 July, the French attacked Pointe Lévis in order to silence the gun battery, but were repulsed by the British detachment stationed there.

The Attempt on the Beauport Shore

On 31 July Wolfe tried a frontal assault on a redoubt just west of the Montmorency River, using grenadiers as his vanguard. They captured the redoubt, but this proved to be an untenable position since the French and Indians could fire into it from higher ground inland. Although other troops were landed, and Wolfe thought of attacking entrenchments farther to the west, he called off the assault without asking Monckton, Murray and Townshend to support him. Montcalm could claim a victory that day. The French lost about 60 men, while Wolfe's casualties were 450 in killed and wounded. Montcalm's lines remained intact, leaving Wolfe to continue looking for the right spot to breach them.

Interlude

Five weeks of apparent stalemate followed, during which Wolfe had his American rangers attack settlements in retaliation for the depredations of armed *habitants* against his outposts. In the interval, Vice-Admiral Saunders was being very effective, laying the groundwork that would break the deadlock, by demonstrating that he could move his smaller ships upstream past Quebec's guns. When Montcalm became aware that ships were taking up positions in the vicinity of Cap Rouge, eighteen kilometres above the town, he feared that Wolfe might cut off his sources of supply stored in the ships at Batiscan. Montcalm ordered Bougainville to see that no British landed on the north shore of the St. Lawrence. By small raids and constant ship movements, Wolfe and Saunders kept Bougainville's mobile force on the move.

On the night of 5 August, Saunders slipped five more ships upstream, and on the 9th five more passed Quebec's guns. By that time Wolfe, recovering from a fever, was debating with his brigadiers over the next move. Meanwhile, Brigadier Murray made two unsuccessful attempts to secure a position on the shore. He landed a detachment at Pointe aux Trembles (now Neuville) on 9

August but after losing 140 men because of stiff French resistance, he withdrew. On the 18th Murray landed at Deschambault and managed to blow up a French ammunition warehouse before he was forced to withdraw.

Private in the Canadian Militia, from an engraving of 1758.

September arrived, and the fleet could not risk being icebound in the St. Lawrence; the vessels had to reach the open ocean before winter set in. The brigadiers advocated landing in force in the vicinity of Cap Rouge and marching for Quebec from there. Wolfe agreed, and began investigating a practical landing site. He admitted that even if he could dislodge Montcalm from the Beauport shore, he would still have to cross the St. Charles River to reach Quebec, and bridges were always bottlenecks.

Wolfe could concentrate nearly all his troops for one strong thrust, and such a move offered the best hope of forcing Montcalm to come out from behind his defences and fight. Once Wolfe's army stood between Quebec and Montcalm's sources of supply, he would have no choice but to try and dislodge the British army.

On 3 September, Wolfe evacuated the camp beside the Montmorency, left only token forces on the Ile d'Orléans and Pointe Lévis, and moved the bulk of his army to the south shore of the St. Lawrence opposite Quebec. By the 5th the stream of redcoats was flowing westwards to the spot where the transport vessels were stationed, opposite Cap Rouge. Then Wolfe discovered the path that ran diagonally upwards from the beach to the cliff-top, at l'Anse au Foulon (now Wolfe's Cove – the path is now the steep road, Cote Gilmour, with a commemorative plaque at the top).

Cap Rouge was some eighteen kilometres west of the city wall, but l'Anse au Foulon was barely three. A French outpost stood at the top of the path, but a few men could overpower its defenders. To the west of this outpost stood the Samos battery, but again a small force could put it out of action. At last Wolfe had his plan, and the means to implement it, thanks to Saunders' work. The combined operation – cooperation of the navy with the army – was destined to proceed smoothly. Luck, too, was on Wolfe's side.

Preliminary to the Battle

Saunders, remaining opposite Quebec with ships of the line too large to proceed upstream, created a diversion to suggest to Montcalm that Wolfe's true objective was still the Beauport shore. The ruse succeeded, for Montcalm remained at the Beauport site with his regulars, and Vaudreuil with his militia. The French commander was aware that the British were planning a move, but he was convinced that Wolfe was staging a feint upstream to make him reduce his strength at Beauport prior to the attack there.

While Saunders was busy deceiving Montcalm, Rear-Admiral Charles Holmes commanded the fleet above Quebec. The first wave of troops — light infantry under Lieutenant-Colonel Willian Howe — would travel in oared boats to l'Anse au Foulon, followed by more troops on transport vessels who would transfer to the boats when they returned empty from the shore. Timing was crucial, for the lower St. Lawrence was tidal. The landing had to be staged taking into account local currents as well as the tide. The other requirement was silence. The legend that Wolfe was reciting Grey's *Elegy in a Country Churchyard* as his boat approached the beach is romantic nonsense.

The Element of Luck

The path Wolfe chose was not entirely satisfactory since it would have made a poor line of retreat had Montcalm arrived in strength before Wolfe had a substantial force on the heights. However, fortune smiled on Wolfe, and the element of surprise prevailed. In fact, the French played into Wolfe's hands through their own plans. On the night of 12 September they intended running boatloads of supplies down river under cover of darkness. Quebec was in need of more provisions and military stores. Sentries posted along the shore had been warned not to challenge too loudly lest they alert the British in the vicinity of Cap Rouge. The plan was cancelled but no one bothered to inform the sentries.

At about 2.00 a.m. what did move down river was a flotilla of small boats carrying the first wave of Wolfe's army. The landing party was Howe's 1,800 light infantrymen, and in the lead boat were twenty-four volunteers led by Captain William Delaune. Captain James Chadds, Royal Navy, was responsible for seeing the men safely ashore. Several versions recount how a French-speaking Scots Highlander (called by more than one name) responded to the sentries, assuring them that the passers-by were loyal to France. While all this was taking place, Saunders' ships staged a diversion, which held Montcalm's attention until nearly daylight.

Between 4.00 and 4.30 a.m. the lead boats touched the beach at l'Anse au Foulon, rather farther east than Wolfe intended but still very close to the objective. While Delaune's volunteers moved west-wards searching for the path, Howe led his light infantrymen straight at the slope, grasping branches and bushes to pull themselves upwards, a remarkable feat best appreciated by walking east of the Quebec Yacht Club along the lower road.

Once on the Plains of Abraham, the light infantrymen turned west to deal with the outpost near the top of the path. In command of the outpost was Louis Du Pont Duchambon de Vergor, who in 1755 surrendered Beauséjour to Robert Monckton (who at that moment was heading for l'Anse au Foulon with his division). Vergor had not improved, or his men might have been doing their sleeping by day. Once more a French-speaking Highlander lulled the enemy by assuring sentries that nothing was amiss. Vergor did manage to send an orderly to warn the town before Howe's men overran his outpost. By that time the volunteers under Delaune had found the path at l'Anse au Foulon, and were followed by men from

Battle on the Plains of Abraham, 13 September 1759.

78

Murray's division. At some point Wolfe landed, although how close to the start is not apparent. When Howe's light infantrymen were hurrying from Vergor's position to deal with the Samos battery, Wolfe called them back. Having been told that some Frenchmen had arrived on the Plains of Abraham, Wolfe ordered Howe's men to take up a position there. However, the French at the Samos battery had seen the redcoats coming, which was sufficient for them to spike their guns and flee.

The landing and ascent to the plains were not accomplished without casualties. Militia and Indians quickly stationed themselves in the woods around the plains and began firing on the troops, and before they had abandoned the Samos battery the gunners had hit two ships. Thus the scene was hardly tranquil as the steady stream of redcoats moved up the path from the beach and sailors hauled up two 6-pounder cannon — all the artillery Wolfe would have for the battle. Wolfe was forming his men up, backs to the river at first. He ordered them to lie down on their arms to afford them some protection until Montcalm was ready to fight. Each side fired off cannons as a way of rattling the other.

Montcalm reacted quickly once he learned of the redcoats on the Plains of Abraham. He moved his five regiments of regulars and part of the militia and marines into the city and on to the plains, expecting Vaudreuil to follow promptly with more militia. He sent a courier to Bougainville with orders to join him with all speed — a message Bougainville received at 8.00 a.m.

Montclam's decision to give battle as early in the day as he did suggests questionable judgement. He did have reason to react quickly because Quebec did not have enough provisions to withstand a long siege. He told his subordinates that he did not want to allow Wolfe time to reinforce his position before striking him. At the same time, Wolfe was unable to contemplate a long siege since winter would soon be approaching and for the fleet time was running out. Nonetheless Montcalm's skirmishers were doing well, and he could have afforded to wait at least two hours. This might have allowed more of Vaudreuil's militia to join him on the plains, and for Bougainville to arrive from Cap Rouge. Montcalm was impatient, perhaps because he was infuriated that Wolfe had outwitted him, and he went ahead. At 10.00 a.m. on 13 September the ten-minute battle began.

The Battle

Numerically, the two armies that faced each other were about equal, the 4,500 British in scarlet, the French regulars in white and the militiamen in grey. The British were from the 15th, 28th, 35th, 43rd, 47th, 58th Regiments of Foot, the 2nd and 3rd battalions of the 60th Royal Americans, the 78th Fraser Highlanders, and the Louisbourg Grenadiers. All were regulars — highly trained professional soldiers. Most had been sent from Britain, but the Royal American Regiment was of Provincials. (The 2nd battalion had been raised in New York, and the 3rd in Nova Scotia). Wolfe had used his American rangers as raiders, but he left them stationed along the south shore of the St. Lawrence. He did not think they would be suitable for what he knew would be a European-style battle where steadiness was the key to success.

The French force contained the regulars of the five regiments in the garrison, perhaps 2,000 men. The rest of Montcalm's army was made up of *troupes de la marine* — colonial regulars — and

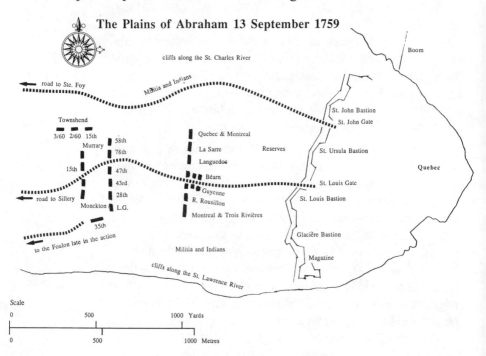

Positions of the two armies at the start of the battle. The armies clashed approximately between Cartier and de Salaberry Streets.

militia and Indians.

Wolfe's foot soldiers were under orders not to fire until the French were within musket range, perhaps forty metres, although details vary as to the distance. Legend tells of one spectacular volley, but the military historian, C.P. Stacey, author of *Quebec 1759*, thought it not possible. The line of troops was far too long for one coordinated volley. The battlefield was about twice as wide as the present Battlefields Park. The British and French lines straddled the present Grand Allée. The right end of the British line was close to the site of the prison, while Montcalm's line was on higher ground called Buttes à Neveu, where the two Martello towers built in the early nineteenth century now stand. The actual battle took place approximately between the current Cartier and de Salaberry streets.

In Stacey's opinion, because of the length of the line, the British fired by platoons, except for the centre, which was narrow enough to fire as one unit. The volleys were preceeded by grape shot discharged by artillerymen operating the two 6-pounders. This caused some disorder in the French line, where the centre was advancing more rapidly than the right or left, rendering it isolated and vulnerable. After firing a volley, the British line advanced to get clear of the blinding smoke, and it remained intact. The French line, now falling apart, was firing with little effect, and doing less damage than the skirmishers operating from the woods. The French soon fled pell mell back towards the town. The British were in hot pursuit, especially the Highlanders of the 78th, who shouted as Highlanders had done at Culloden. Here, as there, they threw away their empty muskets and charged with their broadswords, suffering unnecessary casualties.

Behind them Wolfe lay dead, felled by the second or third shot he had taken. Early in the fray he had been shot in the wrist, but a body wound killed him. His second-in-command, Brigadier Robert Monckton, wounded although not seriously, was unable to take over, and the command devolved upon Brigadier George Townshend. Alarmed that Bougainville might be approaching, Townshend called off the pursuit of Montcalm's fleeing troops and concentrated on reforming the army on the Plains of Abraham. One of Wolfe's biographers, Duncan Grinnell-Milne, questioned the soundness of Townshend's conduct. He had plenty of other troops to deal with Bougainville, such as the 48th Regiment, which had been in reserve at the time of the battle. If Townshend had allowed the pursuit to continue, the troops could have blocked the road at the Cap Rouge River, thereby preventing the escape to Montreal of a large part of Montcalm's army.

Stacey is kinder to Townshend. Communication took time, and he did not learn of Wolfe's death and Monckton's incapacity immediately. He did the best he could in a situation where he did not know exactly what was happening, although failure to cut off Vaudreuil and the French army had preserved it to fight another campaign.

Casualties were heavy on both sides. Townshend reported 600 lower ranks and 58 officers killed. The regiment that took the most punishment was the 78th Fraser Highlanders with 168 casualties, mainly because of their reckless charge against the fleeing French.

Death of Wolfe by Benjamin West. The artist showed Major Robert Rogers on the left above the crouching Indian, wearing a forage cap of the day. Rogers was not at the battle, but with his rangers on the other side of the St. Lawrence River.

Vaudreuil thought that some 600 lower ranks and 44 officers were dead or wounded, among them Montcalm. Many of the British soldiers had been wounded during the skirmishing before the battle, while nearly all the French casualties were suffered in the short fight.

In Quebec, Vaudreuil was now in command; Montcalm lay dying from a battle wound. Vaudreuil called a council of war to decide the next move. Intendant Bigot favoured another attempt to dislodge Wolfe's army from the Plains of Abraham, but most of Vaudreuil's subordinates favoured withdrawal to Montreal, to save the army in order to fight another day. During the night of the 13th, Vaudreuil set out with about 3,000 able-bodied troops, north on

Death of Montcalm, by Desfontaines, from a print in the Public Archives of Canada.

the road to Charlesbourg, which still lay open to him. He swung west to make use of a ford over the St. Charles River, and passed along a winding route to Ancienne Lorette, where his force crossed the Cap Rouge River.

By this time Bougainville was already on his way to Montreal. Upon receiving Montcalm's message at Cap Rouge in the morning, he had started for the Plains of Abraham, and he was close enough by ten o'clock that morning to hear the battle. His scouts soon warned him that his side was in retreat, and that Townshend had moved two battalions facing the road to Ste. Foy. At that Bougainville withdrew and resolved to take his army to Montreal for safety.

While waiting for Quebec to decide to surrender, Townshend had his troops move 100 more pieces of artillery from l'Anse au Foulon to the Plains of Abraham. The city capitulated on 18 September, and the British army occupied it. Vice-Admiral Saunders stayed for a time, landing stores and provisions for the garrison of 7,500 men under Brigadier Murray would remain over the winter. Then, leaving two sloops and three armed schooners behind, Saunders sent a powerful squadron to Halifax with orders to return to Quebec as early as possible in the spring. On 18 October, with four ships of the line and some smaller vessels, Saunders dropped down river bound for England

Wolfe's victory of September 1759 was followed on 28 April 1760 by a British defeat, an encounter described as more decisive than that fought seven months earlier. At the April battle, the Chevalier de Lévis, Montcalm's successor, appeared on the road from Ste. Foy with some 5,000 men. Brigadier Murray's garrison had been weakened by illness during the winter, and he had fewer effectives than Lévis. Murray took up the position that Montcalm had chosen, and in the battle he was outflanked and forced to retire back inside Quebec to avoid too many casualties. Lévis laid siege to the town until 9 May when the first British ship of the spring, the *Lowestoft*, arrived, followed shortly by more of the fleet from Halifax. Lévis retired to Montreal, where the French would soon be confronted by British armies advancing from Quebec, Lake Champlain and Lake Ontario.

The loss of Quebec, even more than Louisbourg or Carillon, was the beginning of the end for New France. The French still held

Montreal, but the British were holding Quebec and blocking the St. Lawrence. Montreal could no longer be supplied or reinforced and its surrender was only a matter of months.

Battle of the Thousand Islands, 1760   6

The last battle fought by the French for New France occured around a small island at the head of the Galops Rapids in the St. Lawrence River. A gallant display the losers made of it. On the French side, three men stand out as the heros of the time – Captain Pierre Pouchot, Commodore René Hypolite Pépin *dit* La Force, and Captain Pierre Boucher de Labroquerie. Pouchot was a regular officer in the Régiment de Béarn and a skilled military engineer who came from Grenoble, France. La Force and Labroquerie were Canadians. La Force, a fine sailor and Governor Vaudreuil's naval commander on the Great Lakes, had spent part of his childhood at Fort Niagara, where his father was the storekeeper. Pouchot had been the commandant of Fort Niagara in August 1759, and he surrendered that post to Sir William Johnson after British troops and Indians ambushed reinforcements on the way to relieve his small garrison.

Now, in August 1760, Pouchot was again facing a British army against impossible odds. The setting was Ile Royale (Chimney Island, just inside the New York boundary), where the French had begun constructing the new Fort Lévis, named in honour of Montcalm's successor as commander-in-chief, the Chevalier Gaston François de Lévis. The island had steep cliffs and because of its proximity to the rapids, ships firing on it would have to manoeuvre upstream, sailing in one at a time.

The British commander-in-chief, Jeffrey Amherst, was planning

View of Fort Oswegatchie (formerly La Présentation) in 1765, redrawn by Colonel F.C. Curry. The fort was refitted by the British and renamed in 1760.

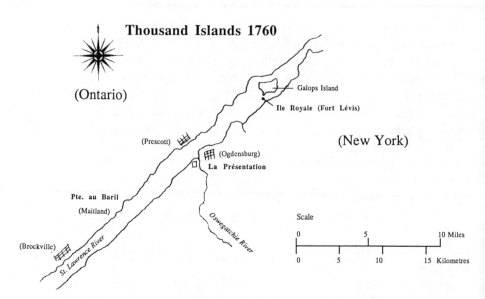

The St. Lawrence River showing the relationship between Pointe au Baril, La Présentation and Ile Royale, and to the modern communities.

a three-pronged attack on Montreal. That city, Fort Lévis, a shipyard on the north shore of the St. Lawrence at Pointe au Baril (east of Maitland), Fort La Présentation (Ogdensburg, New York) and Detroit and some inland posts, were the only places still in French hands. One British army was moving on Montreal from Quebec City, another was advancing from Lake Champlain, while the main force 10,000 strong and commanded by Amherst, had formed up at Oswego and was moving down the St. Lawrence. Captain Pouchot had been sent to New York City as a prisoner of war after he surrendered Fort Niagara. When Pouchot was freed through a prisoner exchange, Lévis sent him to take command of Fort Lévis with orders to delay Amherst's advance as long as possible. France's only hope of saving Montreal was by taking on each British army separately.

Pouchot began by evacuating Pointe au Baril and Fort La Présentation. Both were on low ground and vulnerable to Amherst's guns. In command at La Présentation was a soldier-priest, the Sulpician Abbé François Piquet; the fort had been built in 1749 as a mission

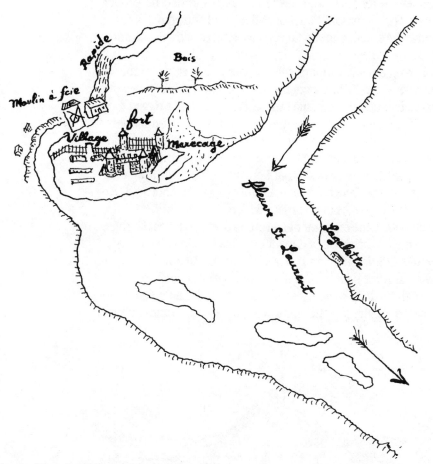

La Présentation   1749

Moulin à scie

Rapide

Bois

Village

fort

Marécage

fleuve St Laurent

Lagalette

Sketch of La Présentation as it looked soon after it was opened in 1749 as a mission to the Iroquois Indians who hunted in the neighbourhood.

to the Iroquois Indians who hunted in the area. Abbé Piquet, like Abbé Le Loutre at Beauséjour, incited his converts to attack British settlements to the south. Despite the priest's protestations — he liked a good fight — Pouchot sent him to Montreal with other civilians for safety.

Chevalier de Lévis' plan for Fort Lévis called for 200 cannon, stone walls and a garrison of 2,500 men. What Pouchot actually had was a small fort of oak logs and five cannon that were difficult to manoeuvre for they were lashed to logs and had no proper carriages. For a garrison, Pouchot had 200 soldiers, most of them militiamen. As well, Captain La Force was there with his flagship, the corvette *l'Iroquoise*, 160 tons with ten 12-pounder guns, schooner-rigged with square sails on her top masts. His subordinate was Captain Labroquerie, in command of the corvette *l'Outaouaise*, about the same size as *l'Iroquoise* but rigged as a brigantine and with one 18-pounder as well as ten 12-pounders. Some 200 sailors and voyageurs manned the two corvettes. Both had been built in the shipyard at Pointe au Baril. The armament and the small garrison suggested that Pouchot could do little against Amherst, but the French officer was stubborn and resourceful. He resolved to carry out Lévis' orders with all his might.

The corvettes, the remnant of La Force's fleet, patrolled the river, while a small detachment of Canadian militia kept watch on Ile aux Chevreuils (Carleton Island) 100 kilometres upstream. On 1 August, La Force's ship *l'Iroquoise* ran aground near Pointe au Baril. With the help of many small boats built at La Présentation by Abbé Piquet, the corvette was towed off the bottom and caulked.

The shipyard at Pointe au Baril (Maitland, Ontario) in 1759. Artist John C. Lamontagne has reconstructed the shipyard and stockade as it may have looked.

Part of her keel was replaced in the shipyard at La Présentation, but she leaked so badly that Pouchot had her beached under the protection of his guns in Fort Lévis. Labroquerie would have to do what he could against Amherst by himself.

General Amherst, appointed commander-in-chief after the death of Wolfe on the Plains of Abraham, had had his men working for a year, stockpiling supplies at Oswego and building whaleboats, fairly good craft for shooting the rapids of the St. Lawrence. All told, some 900 whaleboats were built to carry Amherst's regulars, militia from the northern colonies, Indian allies under Sir William Johnson, and supplies that included 100 siege guns. The small boats would be escorted by two snows – two-masted square-riggers – the *Mohawk* and the *Onondaga*. Both vessels had been started at Fort Niagara by Pouchot and finished by the British after the fort was captured. These armed ships were commanded by Joshua Loring, who in 1745 had advised Governor Shirley of Massachusetts that Louisbourg could be captured. Some small row galleys, each of which had a single gun, were commanded by Colonel George Williamson, an artillery officer from Halifax.

By 7 August 1760 Amherst's advance guard set out, led by the two snows. On Ile aux Chevreuils the French who were keeping a lookout took off in a row galley when they sighted the snows. The *Mohawk* and the *Onondaga* gave chase. The French rowed into the north channel and disappeared among the islands. The snows were soon hopelessly lost. Captain Loring could find neither the French boat nor a way back to the main channel through the maze of islands. Later the crews named this part of the river 'Lost Channel' in memory of their predicament, a name that has been retained.

While the snows were lost, the rest of the advance guard—armed row galleys and whaleboats loaded with light infantrymen, grenadiers and rangers – sailed along the south channel, crossed the open water below the island group now known as the Brockville Narrows, and on the evening of 16 August they occupied the deserted Pointe au Baril and built a gun battery facing the river.

On Ile Royale Captain Pouchot heard three shots from the corvette *l'Outaouaise*, which was anchored below Pointe au Baril – Captain Labroquerie's signal that the British were in sight. Then the naval officer weighed anchor and sailed upstream determined to do all the damage he could when Amherst's main fleet appeared. He was

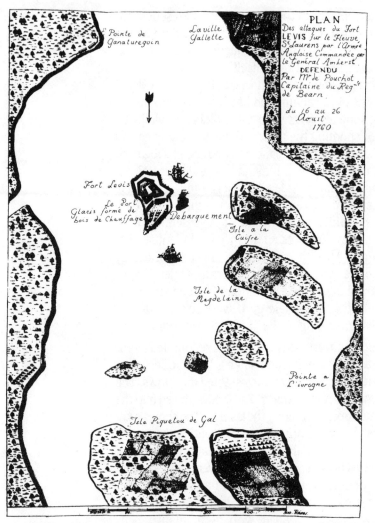

PLAN
Des attaques du Fort
LEVIS fur le Fleuve,
St Laurens par l'Armée
Angloise Commandée par
le Général Amherst.
DEFENDU
Par Mr de Pouchot
Capitaine du Reg.t
de Bearn.

du 16 au 26
Aoust
1760

L'Pointe de
Ganaturegoin

La ville
Gallette

Fort Lévis

Le Port
Glacis formé de
bois de Chauffage

Debarquement

Isle à la
Cuifre

Isle de la
Magdelaine

Pointe à
L'ivrogne

Isle Piquetou de Gal

Contemporary plan of Fort Lévis on Ile Royale showing the nearby islands and the positions of the attacking ships.

already in trouble. The breeze was light, the current against him, and his ship was short of canvas because not enough had been available for enough sails. The first boat approaching was a light gig – a small rowing craft with a sail that was ordinarily used as a tender to take the commanding officer to and from shore.

In the gig, which was sailing rapidly along aided by both wind and current, was Colonel George Williamson. He was leading five row galleys, each carrying a single mounted gun. One galley had a howitzer which threw shells. The others had brass 12-pounders that fired grape and round shot. With the snows *Mohawk* and *Onondaga* still muddling their way through the islands, the galleys were the only protection for the troops on the whaleboats.

Labroquerie had all he could do to tack upstream against the current. The ship was almost immobile while Williamson's little fleet could change direction readily. *L'Outaouaise's* ten 12-pounders were along her sides, and she had to lay off slowly before she was in a position to fire a broadside at the oncoming small boats. Colonel Williamson had his galleys fan out and shelter fore and aft in *l'Outaouaise's* blind spots. All opened fire, pouring a hail of grape shot and shells upon the corvette while her crew tried valiantly to manhandle her round into firing position.

Wounded men fell, and splintered timbers crashed down upon her deck. The ship fired some seventy-two rounds in spite of her difficulties, and two of the row galleys were damaged. Her rigging in splinters, canvas in shreds, the corvette drifted helplessly

View of the encounter between Colonel Williamson's armed row galleys and Labroquerie's ship l'Outaouaise off la Présentation in August 1760.

towards the north shore within range of the battery the British gunners had set up at Pointe au Baril. Now the shore guns joined the row galleys in firing on *l'Outaouaise*.

For three hours the crew of the corvette fought on, blood from the wounded and dead rendering the deck slippery and dangerous for the still able-bodied men. At length, wounded himself and losing blood, Labroquerie agreed to surrender his ship and he ordered her colours struck. Colonel Williamson came aboard with an escort. The captain handed over his sword, collapsed at the victor's feet, and was taken off to a surgeon. Pierre de Labroquerie had fired the last shots of the war from a French ship.

By 19 August, Amherst's entire expedition had reached Pointe au Baril, except for the snows *Mohawk* and *Onondaga*, still trying to make their way out of the Thousand Islands. The battered corvette *l'Outaouaise* had been towed to Pointe au Baril and given a hasty refurbishing and new canvas. She was renamed the *Williamson* in honour of her captor, and her new commanding officer was Captain Patrick Sinclair, a Scot trained on the herring fleets of the North Sea. On the 20th Amherst divided his flotilla into two lines, one moving along the north shore, the other along the south, sheltering in bays, as far as possible from Pouchot's cannon on Ile Royale.

Pierre Labroquerie, now a prisoner of war, watched sadly at the practicality of the British. Painful indeed was the sight of his own ship sailing towards Ile Royale to draw Pouchot's fire and protect the whaleboats. The new *Williamson* (formerly *l'Outaouaise*) was hit forty-eight times during the day, and one row galley was sunk. From his vantage point beside a gun, Pouchot recognized many of the officers, since they had been at the capture of Fort Niagara. Most exchanged pleasantries as they passed by in their boats. Some of the gunners went ashore or to nearby islands, taking cannon and setting up batteries from which to fire upon Pouchot and his little band of defenders inside Fort Lévis.

Commodore La Force was aboard his disabled flagship *l'Iroquoise* ready to defend her with muskets. The corvette lay on her side, guns to port dug into the bottom, guns to starboard pointing heavenward – all equally useless. Before long Pouchot ordered La Force to abandon his plan to stay with his ship and he sent out four small boats to bring the commodore and his 100 sailors to help in the defence of Fort Lévis. By evening the sails of the long overdue *Mohawk* and *Onondaga* were in sight. At dusk Amherst called a ceasefire for the night. The crew of the *Williamson* began to plug up the holes made by Pouchot's gunners during the day.

At dawn on the 20th the *Williamson* resumed her firing on Fort Lévis, joined now by the *Mohawk* and the *Onondaga*. Among them the three vessels sported fifty guns to Pouchot's five comparable cannon, yet the worthy French artillery officer's gunners put all three ships out of action. They sank the *Williamson* and the

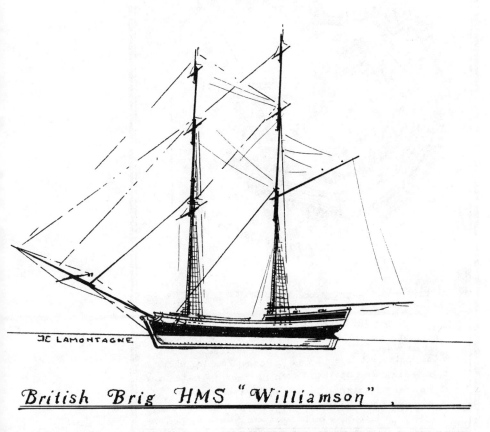

JC LAMONTAGNE

British Brig HMS "Williamson"

Sketch of the H.M.S. Williamson, *formerly* l'Outaouaise, *which was captured off Pointe au Baril in August 1760.*

Onondaga. The *Mohawk* ran aground and was battered to pieces. Afterward the batteries on the shore and on nearby islands kept up a steady fire, raining shells and cannon balls on the helpless

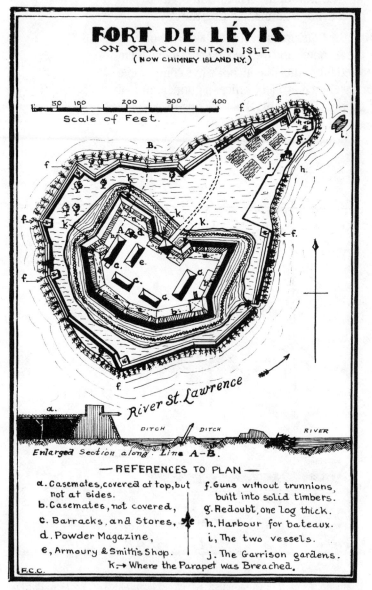

FORT DE LÉVIS
ON ORACONENTON ISLE
(NOW CHIMNEY ISLAND N.Y.)

Scale of Feet.

B.

River St. Lawrence

Enlarged Section along Line A-B.

DITCH   DITCH   RIVER

— REFERENCES TO PLAN —

a. Casemates, covered at top, but not at sides.
b. Casemates, not covered,
c. Barracks, and Stores,
d. Powder Magazine,
e. Armoury & Smith's Shop.
f. Guns without trunnions, built into solid timbers.
g. Redoubt, one log thick.
h. Harbour for bateaux.
i. The two vessels.
j. The Garrison gardens.
k.→ Where the Parapet was Breached.

F.C.C.

Plan of Fort Lévis, the 'Gibralter of the upper St. Lawrence'. The fort was still under construction when Amherst attacked it, and it was never completed.

defenders. When there was no indication that resistance was nearing an end, in desperation Amherst ordered hot shot. For nearly three full days the siege continued unrelentingly.

On 24 August Pouchot was out of ammunition, and his garrison could do no more. Also, with so many fires burning in Ile Royale, and his force of able-bodied men so reduced, he had no hope of putting out the blazes set by British hot shot. He still had a good supply of powder and he was worried that the fires might reach it and blow the survivors to meet their maker. Pouchot was also wounded, struck by falling logs and suffering from many abrasions. He had made a gallant last stand, and he had no cause to be ashamed when he asked Amherst for terms. Amherst readily agreed to accord Pouchot the honours of war – the right to march out and surrender formally.

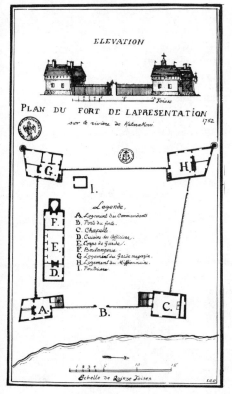

Elevation and interior layout of Fort de La Présentation in 1752.

When Amherst entered Fort Lévis he was quite surprised at how few men were inside and he enquired where Pouchot had hidden his garrison. 'You have my garrison,' Pouchot supposedly replied.

Both men, both professional soldiers, were in high spirits as Amherst chided Pouchot for the carelessness of his gunners. 'They might have shot me, ' he complained. Pouchot solemnly apologized, a twinkle in his eye.

The casualty lists are difficult to assess. Amherst reported British losses as 26 killed and 47 wounded, but he may not have included his militia. At the time British officers tended to report only the losses sustained by regular troops. Pouchot reported French losses as 375 killed or wounded, and his estimate is probably correct since his force consisted mainly of militia and the crews of the two corvettes. Only about 25 of the force that defended Fort Lévis on Ile Royale and of the crew aboard *l'Outaouaise* had escaped death or injury.

The battle was over but that was not the end of the delay caused by Pouchot's stubborn last stand. Amherst remained at Fort Lévis four days, organizing his flotilla for the journey down the rapids. The gun batteries around Ile Royale had to be dismantled, and Fort Lévis repaired and renamed Fort William Augustus, the given names of the Duke of Cumberland, the commander-in-chief of the British army and younger son of King George II. Three of the

Chimney Island, N.Y. (Ile Royale) as it looks today. The cliffs are less formidable now, because the water level was raised during construction of the St. Lawrence Seaway.

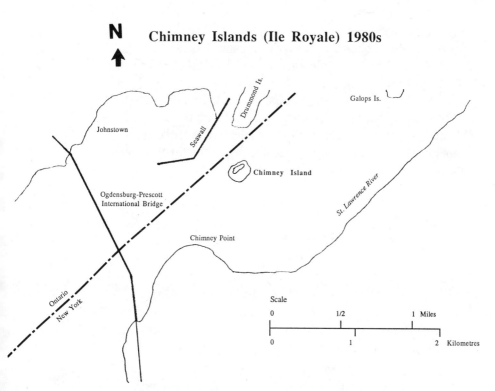

N ↑ Chimney Islands (Ile Royale) 1980s

The position of Chimney Island, N.Y. relative to the international bridge and other modern Seaway installations.

battered ships near Ile Royale were refloated and repaired for patrol duty from Fort William Augustus to Fort Niagara. Amherst had no intention of leaving the rear exposed. When the flotilla set off, a British garrison remained behind in Fort William Augustus.

The journey down the rapids took a greater toll of Amherst's men than the siege of Fort Lévis. He reported the loss of 46 boats and that 84 men drowned. Once again Pouchot's estimates were higher, for he reported that 336 men drowned. His figure probably included militia and prisoners of war. Pouchot's last stand had delayed Amherst's army more than a week, but it did not help Montreal. The British forces converging from Quebec and Lake Champlain waited for Amherst's arrival, instead of attacking the city independently. When Amherst's expedition was finally outside Montreal on 6 September, the French garrison asked for terms. Two days later the city surrendered. Pouchot, La Force and Labroquerie and the other survivors of the Battle of the Thousand islands were sent to New York City as prisoners of war. Later, Pouchot was sent to France. La Force and Labroquerie were allowed to return to Quebec. Although the peace treaty was not signed until 10 February 1763, when the Seven Years' War ended in Europe, New France virtually became a British possession with the surrender of Montreal. It was henceforth known as the Province of Quebec, although it was peopled by Canadians and sometimes called Canada.

Signal Hill 1762

7

Signal Hill in St. John's is one place in Newfoundland that can be called a battle ground, and it is a fine one to visit. The hill portion is a national historic park. Having one recognizable battle ground, however, does not imply a lack of conflicts. In a sense all the parts of the island that were inhabited in the seventeenth century were battle grounds. A fish war was in progress, and the chief contenders were Britain and France. The exact year that Europeans began fishing on the Grand Banks is not known. The fishermen wanted to keep their grounds a secret to avoid competition from other countries' fleets. It is known that Basque whalers were in the area in 1420, and by the 1480s fishing fleets from France, Spain, Portugal and Britain were visiting the Grand Banks.

In the early 1500s, Britain founded St. John's as a base for the fishing fleet, but no fortifications were built then. Settlers were not encouraged to live there permanently because Britain's policy was to have the fishing fleets remain migratory. The fishing ships were a source of crews for the Royal Navy in time of war. The Royal Navy was supposed to protect the fleets, but the early 1600s were a time when pirates took their toll. Barbary pirates operating from North Africa captured many ships bound from Newfoundland to the Mediterranean.

In 1662, the French established a shore base for the fishery at Placentia Bay, which they named Plaisance. When in 1689 the War of the League of Augsburg began, hotly contested places were the fur trade posts on Hudson Bay and the Newfoundland fishery. The North American phase of the conflict was called King William's War. In 1696, the enterprising and aggressive Pierre Le Moyne Sieur d'Iberville, fresh from years of contending for the forts on Hudson Bay, arrived at Plaisance to begin a campaign to drive the British out of Newfoundland. He was accompanied by Jacques Testard de Montigny. In November, with an expedition, they marched across the Avalon Peninsula, destroyed the settlement of Ferryland and captured St. John's on 30 December.

In April 1697, the British government commissioned Captain John Norris of the Royal Navy, commander-in-chief of Newfoundland, and placed a small squadron at his disposal. Norris carried Colonel John Gibson and his regiment to recapture the Newfoundland territories seized by d'Iberville and Montigny. When Norris brought Gibson to St. John's harbour they found that the

Avalon Peninsula
Newfoundland

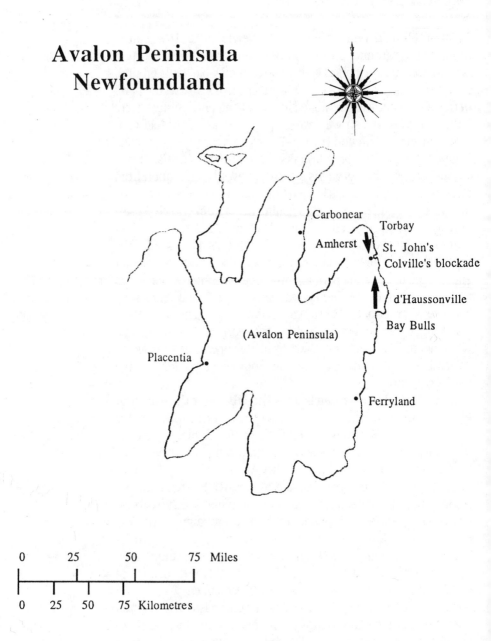

Carbonear

Torbay

Amherst

St. John's

Colville's blockade

d'Haussonville

Bay Bulls

(Avalon Peninsula)

Placentia

Ferryland

| 0 | 25 | 50 | 75 | Miles |

| 0 | 25 | 50 | 75 | Kilometres |

D'Haussonville's attack on St. John's from Bay Bulls; Amherst's relief of St. John's from Torbay.

French had abandoned the base. Gibson's men were the first to garrison the fort, although Fort William had been built in 1693. The fort stood near the junction of Duckworth Street and King's Bridge. A battery was erected on the south shore of the harbour in the narrows close to the mouth.

King William's War concluded with the Treaty of Ryswick, and all territories seized by Britain and France were returned. Britian got Newfoundland and Hudson Bay, and France retained Acadia. Trouble erupted five years later however, in 1702, with the War of the Spanish Succession, of which the North American phase was called Queen Anne's War. Again, several Newfoundland settlements were attacked. The French captured St. John's in January 1709, but abandoned it in April.

The War of the Spanish Succession ended in 1713 with the signing of the Treaty of Utrecht. Britain's ownership of the Hudson Bay Lowland and Newfoundland was confirmed. France was allowed to retain Cape Breton Island and was granted the right to fish in Newfoundland waters and to land to cure fish from Cape Bonavista to Pointe Riche, but she lost Plaisance.

For almost half a century St. John's was a peaceful fishing base, developing mainly along the north shore of the harbour. In the 1740s and 50s, as tension between Britain and France increased, Fort William and the south side battery were rebuilt. Nothing was done to fortify Signal Hill, although it made a superb defensive site, protected on three sides by heights and water, and approachable on only half of its perimeter. It was used for signalling, as early as 1704 and was first called Signal Hill in 1762. Signallers may have stood on Ladies Lookout ridge, the highest point on the hill, where women used to watch for their men returning from the fishing grounds.

By 1762, France had lost her North American colonies except for part of Louisiana and was about to negotiate peace terms. Having little to bargain with, France decided to capture St. John's, to hold in order to secure concessions from Britain. An expedition of 800 men, including 161 Irish mercenaries, sailed from Brest on 8 May 1762. The Irish were to form the core of a battalion to be recruited from among Irish fishermen living in Newfoundland. Two ships of the line, a frigate and two 'flutes' ('en flute' referred to a man of war with reduced armament that was being used as a transport vessel) carried the troops out to sea. The leader of the expedition was Charles-Henri-Louis d'Arsac de Ternay. In command of the land force was Colonel Joseph-Louis-Bernard de Cléron d'Haussonville. The five ships anchored off Bay Bulls, twenty-nine kilometres south of St. John's on 23 June, and hoisted a British flag to avoid warning the garrison.

Stationed at Fort William were the commander, Major Walter Ross, two other officers and forty-seven lower ranks of the 40th Regiment. In the harbour the frigate *Gramont* (a former French ship captured by the British) lay at anchor. When the vessel's commander, Patrick Mouat, learned that d'Haussonville had landed, he sent out a ship's boat that slipped past the French fleet and carried a message for Halifax. Then Mouat scuttled the frigate and joined Major Ross at Fort William. On the 27th d'Haussonville ordered the fort to surrender. Major Ross complied since he was badly outnumbered. The French soon refloated the *Gramont* and put it back in service.

Town and harbour of St. John's, dated 1 June 1831. Artist W. Eagar's lithograph was taken from a vantage point on Signal Hill.

View of Signal Hill as it appeared during the 1840s. By that time the hill was used for signalling, for which it was admirably suited.

A ship bearing the governor of Newfoundland, Thomas Graves, arrived off St. John's. Seeing the French vessels, the ship sailed on to Placentia Bay, where Graves disembarked to take up his duties. He established a temporary headquarters, improved defences, and completed a blockhouse within the walls of a fort the French had built to protect their old base. The new blockhouse was called Castle Graves while the governor remained there. Elsewhere the French carried out the destruction of the British settlements and the facilities for the fishery. They took 460 boats of various sizes and sank them.

News of the French capture of St. John's reached the British at New York City in August. The commander-in-chief of all British forces, General Sir Jeffrey Amherst, was quick to take action to dislodge the French. He ordered Rear Admiral Lord Alexander Colville, at Halifax, to assemble a fleet to blockade St. John's harbour, and placed his brother, Lieutenant-Colonel William Amherst, in command of a land force to be assembled from troops stationed at Louisbourg, Halifax and New York. Colville commandeered ships as they came into Halifax harbour. On 10 August

Colville sailed for Placentia. His flagship was the *Northumberland*, Captain James Cook as master, followed by the 40-gun *Gosport* and the Massachussets provincial vessel *King George* of 20 guns. This fleet was enlarged at Placentia Bay by the 50-gun *Antelope* and the 24-gun *Syren*. In mid-August Colville went off to blockade St. John's.

Lieutenant-Colonel William Amherst arrived off St. John's on 11 September with transports carrying 1,500 British regulars and colonial troops. He landed his men at Torbay on the 13th and brushed aside a French advance party before marching the fifteen kilometres to the vicinity of St. John's. D'Haussonville sent an advance party towards Quidi Vidi harbour and placed some men and a mortar on Signal Hill. The remainder of his force was stationed at Fort William.

Signal Hill, St. John's 1762

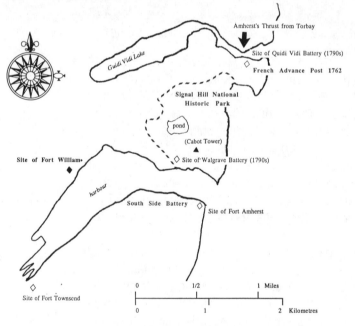

Detail for the expulsion of the French from St. John's by Colonel William Amherst.

This photograph ca. 1900 shows how impregnable Signal Hill was from the sea and what a fine defensive site it made.

Amherst's force made short work of the vanguard at Quidi Vidi and by the 15th he was routing the French from their positions on Signal Hill. The colonel brought his guns across the Quidi Vidi Gut, while Captain Charles McDonell of the 78th (Fraser) Highlanders led his men up the cliff and seized Gibbet Hill, where guns would have an uninterrupted view of the fort and the harbour. Amherst proceeded to move his guns into that favourabale position. That night dense fog enveloped the harbour, and Ternay took advantage of the opportunity the fog afforded to slip his fleet past Colville's blockade and escape. D'Haussonville was left to face the superior British force on his own. On 16 September the British bore down towards Fort William from Signal Hill, and by the 17th they were firing on the fort. The French held out until the 18th before surrendering. France had lost her bid for a bargaining tool in the peace negotiations.

Because Fort William could be attacked so easily from Signal Hill, in the 1770s the British built Fort Townshend, to the west of the older fort, where it could not be fired upon from the hill. During the American Revolution, defences were strengthened, but the fortifications on Signal Hill were not developed to a great extent until the 1790s. The Queen's, Wallace's, Waldgrave, Duke of York's, Quidi Vidi pass and Carronade batteries all date from the early years of the Napoleonic Wars. Signal Hill's fortifications of that era served as a deterrent when a French fleet came towards St. John's in 1796. Barracks were added near Queen's battery in 1832-1833. The last British garrison left St John's in 1870. Signal Hill was thus the last battle of the Seven Years' War fought in North America.

A New Method of MACARONY MAKING, as practiſed at BOSTON in NORTH AMERICA .

Printed for Carington Bowles, Nº 69 in St Pauls Church Yard, London.

Tarring and feathering have come to symbolise the American Revolution. The victim was a Boston commissioner of customs. 'Macarony' was a name used for 18th century English dandies.

The outcome of the Seven Years' War was a major cause of the American Revolution that erupted on 19 April 1775 with the fighting at Concord and Lexington, Massachusetts. The removal of the French presence to the north made people in the Thirteen Colonies feel less dependent on the mother country's military might. The issue that brought matters to a head was whether the British parliament could levy taxes on colonies that did not send representatives to that body. Another grievance was the Quebec Act of 1774 that gave the interior of the continent to the new English colony of Quebec. The colonists had expected to be able to occupy the interior, displacing the Indians at will. They did not want to move into territory where the Roman Catholic religion and French civil law were established.

As 1775 opened, the governor of Canada, Guy Carleton, felt

General Guy Carleton, governor of Canada in 1775-1776. Carleton was knighted for his success in repelling the American rebel invaders.

complacent. He thought he could depend on his loyal militia to protect the province. After all, he had shepherded the Quebec Act through the British Parliament of their behalf. The seigneurs and the clergy were pleased with the act. What Carleton failed to understand was that he had catered to the wrong people. The real leaders were not the seigneurs but the militia captains, who would have been happy to see the privileges of the clergy reduced. As a consequence, when an expedition of Americans was forming on Lake Champlain, Carleton found that few men volunteered for military service. To make matters worse, Carleton had sent the 10th and 52nd Regiments from Quebec to Boston at request of General Thomas Gage, the commander-in-chief in the Thirteen Colonies. That left only two regiments of British regular troops – the 7th Fusiliers and the 26th Foot – to defend Canada.

St. Jean Quebec 1775

8

The battle at Fort St. Jean took place in the opening months of the American Revolution, when two small armies of rebels tried to capture Canada. Log forts had been built at St. Jean and Chambly as early as 1665 by soldiers of the Carignan-Salières Regiment. The forts were two of a number that were constructed along the Richelieu River to guard the route from Lake Champlain — the easiest point of access from the English colonies and the territory of the Iroquois Indians. By 1775 St. Jean was in a neglected state, but Fort Chambly had been rebuilt commencing in 1709. The second fort was of stone, with walls five metres high, and with four bastions that were more than two metres higher. Chambly looked formidable, but the walls were not thick enough to withstand heavy artillery bombardment.

Fort Chambly is a national historic park. Fort St. Jean is the site of the Collège Militaire de St. Jean, where artifacts from the old fort are preserved at a museum. Another historic site related to St. Jean is Ile aux Noix, where Fort Lennox stands in another national · historic park. Early French fortifications dating from 1659 on Ile aux Noix were destroyed by the British in 1760. Fort Lennox was

View of restored Fort Chambly, Fort Chambly National Historic Park, Chambly, Quebec.

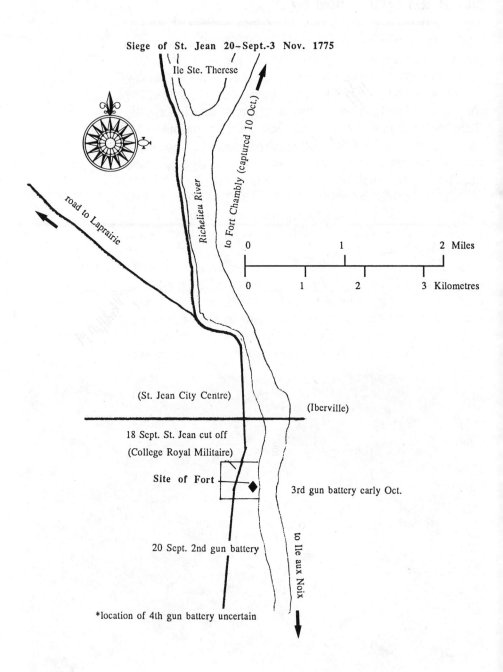

Siege of St. Jean 20–Sept.-3 Nov. 1775

Ile Ste. Therese

Richelieu River

to Fort Chambly (captured 10 Oct.)

road to Laprairie

0   1   2 Miles

0   1   2   3 Kilometres

(St. Jean City Centre)

(Iberville)

18 Sept. St. Jean cut off

(College Royal Militaire)

Site of Fort

3rd gun battery early Oct.

20 Sept. 2nd gun battery

to Ile aux Noix

*location of 4th gun battery uncertain

The actual site of Fort St. Jean is in the grounds of the Collège Royal Militaire, *and is less obvious than the restored forts at Chambly and Ile aux Noix.*

built between 1819 and 1829. All three sites were captured in the autumn of 1775 by American rebels before they occupied Montreal and threatened Quebec City. Fort St. Jean was the scene of a lengthy siege.

In May, Vermont's Green Mountain Boys, led by their big, rough chief, Ethan Allen, with Benedict Arnold and some Massachusetts men, appeared on the shore of Lake Champlain. They captured Forts Ticonderoga and Crown Point from their small, caretaker British garrisons. Afterwards, Arnold stole a schooner that belonged to an absent Loyalist, renamed it the *Liberty*, and with some Massachusetts militia set out for Fort St. Jean. He had heard that a government sloop loaded with supplies was there. The

Benedict Arnold, whose name has come to symbolise a turncoat. After showing great initiative against the British and Canadians, Arnold defected to the British side at West Point, N.Y. in 1780.

schooner arrived and took the small British garrison by surprise. The men surrendered, and Arnold took the sloop, burned some bateaux because he did not have enough men to operate them, and withdrew to Lake Champlain. There he met Ethan Allen, who was determined to outdo him. Allen went north, and learning from a merchant, Joseph Bindon, that some of the 26th Regiment under Major Charles Preston were coming to retake St. Jean, Allen set up an ambush. Bindon met Preston's force but did not warn them of Allen's plan. When Preston arrived at St. Jean, Allen's men lost their nerve and fled in their boats. Preston was convinced that Bindon knew of Allen's intent, but he had kept quiet because he sympathized with the Americans. When some of the soldiers returned to Montreal they put Bindon in the pillory for his omission.

The defences of Montreal were weak, and time did not permit strengthening them. Carleton decided that Fort St. Jean was the strategic place to make a stand against an invasion from the south. A road ran to Laprairie where a ferry operated between there and Montreal. St. Jean would be difficult for an invading army to bypass. Vessels stationed in the Richelieu could intercept any ship entering from Lake Champlain. If an invasion did not materialize, Carleton intended using St. Jean as a base for the recovery of Ticonderoga and Crown Point. Fort St. Jean was just two earthen redoubts, one around the barracks, the other around a stone house. Carleton put Captain John Marr, of the Royal Engineers, in charge of improving the defences. Marr decided to link the two redoubts with a stockade, and to surround the three landward sides with a ditch two metres deep. Beyond the stockade Marr set up rows of pickets. Along the river the fort would be protected by a fleet. Carleton sent Lieutenant William Hunter, of the Royal Navy, to St. Jean to build it. His carpenters began work on a schooner, the *Royal Savage*, and two armed row galleys.

The garrison, under Major Charles Preston, was 662 men – 474 of the 26th Regiment, 90 Canadian volunteers and militia, 38 Royal Artillerymen and 20 Royal Highland Emigrants. The Highlanders belonged to a new regiment of provincials under a regular officer, Lieutenant-Colonel Allan Maclean. Carleton moved his headquarters to Montreal to deal with the emergency at close range, and he sent Maclean to take command of the Quebec City

The schooner Royal Savage *was stationed at Fort St. Jean during the siege. After the fort surrendered the Americans made use of the ship.*

garrison and to prepare the defences there. Also at St. Jean were some Canadians under Sieur de Belestre, a veteran of the Seven Years' War skilled in irregular combat, and some Indians led by François de Lormier and Gilbert Tice, officers in the Indian Department. Fort Chambly, with its unsubstantial stone walls, would be the supply depot for Fort St. Jean.

Spying for the Americans near St. Jean was Remember Baker, a cousin of Ethan Allen. Baker was soon killed by Indians scouting for Preston. They cut off his head and carried it to St. Jean where they mounted it on a pole. The horrified Preston ordered the head taken down and given a decent burial.

The American attack was from two directions. The Lake Champlain force was commanded by Major-General Philip Schuyler (whose mansion is still an Albany landmark), and his second-in-command was Brigadier-General Richard Montgomery, a former British regular. The other force was commanded by Benedict Arnold, and his route lay up the Kennebec River and down the

Major Charles Preston (later Sir Charles) commanded the defenders of St. Jean against rebels led by Richard Montgomery.

Chaudière for a direct approach to Quebec City. Schuyler and Montgomery left Crown Point on 30 August with 1,500 men. Most were from New York, but the Green Mountain Boys, from Vermont, accompanied the expedition, led by another of Ethan Allen's cousin, Seth Warner. The Vermont leaders thought Allen too rash, and gave the command of the regiment he had raised to his more conservative cousin. Arnold's force, of 1,200 New Englanders and Pennsylvanians, left Cambridge, Massachusetts, on 11 September,

Royal Highland Emigrants. The regiment was raised from among Highlanders who had settled in North America. Emigrants who served at the siege of St. Jean had not yet been issued with these uniforms, and were attired in whatever was available in the army stores.

Schuyler was expected to capture Montreal while Arnold took Quebec.

Schuyler's force reached Ile aux Noix on 4 September, travelling in clumsy flat-bottomed boats. Leaving a small detachment to protect his rear, he went on to within three kilometres of St. Jean. Gunners in the fort spotted the boats and began firing, but the Americans kept on coming. Schuyler's troops landed in a swampy area and formed companies. As they started for the fort, Lormier

Major-General Richard Montgomery led the American rebels at the siege of St. Jean. He was a former British regular officer who joined the rebels.

and Tice ambushed them. The Americans took cover, and despite the shooting threw up a breastwork. At length the guns of the fort forced them to withdraw. Four Indians were killed, and Tice and four other Indians were wounded.

Schuyler received a visit from a resident of St. Jean, Moses Hazen, who was acting as a double agent, supplying information to both sides. He warned Schuyler that the Canadians would not rise up and support him. Schuyler then withdrew back to Ile aux Noix. American volunteers kept arriving, and Schuyler found that he had 1,900 men at Ile aux Noix. However, malaria was taking its toll, and many men were not fit to leave their tents.

On 10 September, Brigadier Montgomery set out with 1,000 men, and he sent a detachment under Lieutenant-Colonel Robert Ritzema to take a post north of St. Jean to cut Preston from Montreal.

Ritzema's men fought a skirmish with some Indians and went scurrying back to Montgomery's position. When Montgomery heard a rumour that the *Royal Savage* was about to attack him, he led his men back the sixteen kilometres to Ile aux Noix. Schuyler was now ill, and he was sent on a vessel to Ticonderoga. Montgomery took command, and he returned with his army to St. Jean. He now had 2,000 able-bodied men and a fleet – a schooner, a sloop and two row galleys, each galley with a 13-pounder gun, and ten bateaux. He had enough water craft to keep the *Royal Savage* out of Lake Champlain.

Near Chambly dwelt James Livingston, an American in sympathy with the revolution, who persuaded forty Canadians to join Montgomery. That officer placed them under Major John Brown, a man who had been spying in Canada for months. Brown went forward and captured a supply train bound from Laprairie for St. Jean. Then he occupied an old redoubt on the road. Preston knew that he must dislodge Brown, but the patrol he sent out returned after a short but withering exchange. In the engagement some of Preston's men were wounded.

By the evening of the 18th, the Americans were in control of the west bank of the Richelieu above and below St. Jean, and ready to start their siege. Preston had Lormier slip away to Montreal to alert Carleton. Montgomery sent Brown with a small party to spy on Carleton's movements. Ethan Allen went to Longueuil with some Canadians hoping to attack Montreal, and James Livingston was trying with only limited success, to get more recruits around Chambly. The French Canadians tended to ignore both Carleton's call for volunteers and American blandishments equally.

The siege of Fort St. Jean began on 19 September in driving rain. Brigadier-General Richard Prescott, Carleton's second-in-command, ordered Major Preston to take the offensive, and to consult Belestre because he was experienced in the necessary tactics. Preston made good use of his gunners, since he had plenty of ammunition. To clear a field of fire, he blew up some buildings that blocked the view from the fort. When the Americans began erecting a gun battery less than 400 metres away, Preston kept up fire to interfere with their work. All women and children moved into the fort for safety, and this made 1,300 occupants crammed inside the stockade. Montgomery's men now began work on a battery to the north of the fort. Preston had his fleet moving back and forth between the two Americans positions, covering them with gun fire.

At Longueuil, Ethan Allen, with 120 followers, attempted his foolhardy plan to capture Montreal. He was taken by a party of Indians led by Indian Department officers, and a detachment of the 26th Regiment – news that reached St. Jean on 29 September. The man who accepted Allen's sword was Ensign Peter Warren Johnson of the 26th. (He was a son of Sir William Johnson and a great nephew of Commodore Peter Warren who commanded the naval

Lieutenant-Colonel Allan Maclean, who raised the Royal Highland Emigrants. In 1778 the regiment was placed on the British regular establishment as the 84th Foot.

squadron at Louisbourg in 1745.) The capture of the invincible Ethan Allen inspired many Canadians to enlist in Carleton's militia. He soon found that he had 2,000 volunteers, but he was not yet ready to march to the relief of St. Jean.

While the Americans were distracted, bringing up more heavy artillery from Ticonderoga, part of the St. Jean garrison slipped out and brought in cattle to provide the beleaguered occupants of the fort with fresh meat. Conditions inside the stockade were growing deplorable. Preston reported that because of the shelling the only safe place to sleep was the cellar, but the stench from so many unwashed bodies was overpowering. He preferred to spend the nights pacing in the fresh air. In any event, a full night's sleep was impossible, since bursts of shelling broke out often in the darkness.

Montgomery was working on a third battery, on the east bank opposite St. Jean, which placed Preston in a dangerous dilemma. The new battery could menace the side of the fort which his ships defended. He sent a row galley with a 24-pounder mounted on it against the battery. After a brief exchange the boat was forced to withdraw. Now that the new battery was threatening the fleet, Lieutenant Hunter suggested moving all vessels and boats to between the two redoubts of Fort St. Jean. That way, if they were sunk, the artillery and stores could be salvaged. Without warning the *Royal Savage* was hit and she sank before Hunter could have her brass guns removed. With the ships no longer able to patrol, the fort was more congested than ever because Hunter's crews had to have somewhere to stay.

At last Carleton took steps to relieve st. Jean. He sent orders to Lieutenant-Colonel Maclean to bring a force from Quebec to Sorel and march up the Richelieu. Carleton would assemble another force at Montreal and meet Maclean in front of St. Jean. Maclean took 120 of his Royal Highland Emigrants, 60 of the 7th Regiment, and some Canadian militia. After recruiting along the way he increased his force to 400 men. On St. Helen's Island, in the St. Lawrence, Carleton began assembling 800 Canadian militia, 130 Royal Highland Emigrants and 80 Indians.

Meanwhile, James Livingston suggested to Major John Brown that they attack Fort Chambly. Livingston had recruited some Canadians, and Brown agreed to use the men he had assembled. With between 200 and 500 men – records vary – they prepared

Likeness of Ethan Allen. After forming his Green Mountain Boys, Ethan was deemed too rash to lead them to Canada. Command went to Seth Warner, but Allen accompanied Montgomery's expedition as a volunteer.

their siege. Inside the fort, under the command of Major the Honourable Joseph Stopford, were 6 officers, 5 sergeants, 3 drummers and fifers, and 62 other ranks of the 7th Regiment, and five Royal Artillerymen. Many women and children were there, some related to men at Fort St. Jean. Brown and Livingston's men began firing on the fort on 16 October, and Stopford surrendered on the 18th, which was almost an act of cowardice. He had plenty of ammunition, and the enemy had not done much damage. Worse, Stopford did not destroy the provisions and ammunition, a welcome windfall to the invaders.

On the 20th, two Americans with a flag of truce arrived at St. Jean with a message from Stopford. He asked Preston to allow some American boats to pass down to Chambly to remove the women and children. Stopford and all the men would be coming past on foot on their way to a prison in American-controlled territory. The boats returned on the 21st, and Montgomery let the women whose men were in the St. Jean garrison disembark with their children. The rest would accompany the prisoners-of-war. Preston was now cut off from Montreal and the morale of the Americans soared. They had been ready to retire when they heard that Ethan Allen had been captured.

At last Carleton was ready to come to the aid of St. Jean. His 1,200 man force embarked in bateaux, but off Longueuil he was fired on by Seth Warner and 350 of his Green Mountain Boys, who

Fort Chambly as it appeared in 1815. This aquatint by Colonel J. Bouchette was engraved by J. and C. Walker.

Carleton reviewed his troops in Montreal's Place d'Armes before setting out to relieve St. Jean. He turned back after a brush with a small force under Ethan Allen.

had obtained one of Fort Chambly's field guns. Unnerved, Carleton withdrew and he sent a message to inform Maclean that he would not be joining him on the Richelieu. Maclean's own force had been weakened by desertion, but he tried to push his way on to St. Denis. After skirmishing with some of Brown and Livingston's men, he turned back. He was badly outnumbered and without Carleton's support he had no hope of reaching St. Jean.

There, the Americans stepped up their fire. They added a fourth gun battery, but Preston's reports do not show where it stood. The guns of the new battery began firing on 1 November, causing few casualties but destroying some provisions. Preston figured that if he put everyone on two-thirds rations he could hold out eight more days in the hope that Carleton's reinforcements would arrive. Montgomery sent Preston a messenger who informed him that Carleton had withdrawn. When Montgomery suggested that he surrender, Preston retorted that the report on Carleton might be false. He might agree to capitulate in four days if no reinforcements came. Montgomery informed Preston that if he did not surrender at once he would not be accorded the honours of war. At that Preston's resolve crumbled, and the two commanders signed terms on 2 November. On the 3rd the British troops marched out of the fort after a siege of fifty-five days, and followed the Chambly garrison south as prisoners-of-war.

Carleton evacuated Montreal on 11 November and Montgomery occupied the town on the 12th. On the 14th Benedict Arnold appeared outside Quebec's walls, and withdrew up the St. Lawrence until Montgomery could join him. They began besieging Quebec on 6 December. On the 31st they attacked and were defeated by Maclean, who took more than 400 prisoners. Montgomery was killed and Arnold, wounded, was removed to Montreal. The rebels ended their siege on 6 May when reinforcements arrived by sea from Britain, and they withdrew to Sorel. A force that attacked the American outpost at the Cedars, above Montreal, captured it and took 500 more prisoners on 20 May. On 15 June Arnold evacuated Montreal and by the 18th both American forces were at St. Jean in full retreat. Although he did not recover Ticonderoga and Crown Point that season, Carleton did drive the rebels out of Canada. For that he was knighted, although his critics felt that he might have showed more determination and courage, especially after the brush with the Green Mountain Boys.

Carleton erred in allowing prisoners taken at Quebec on 31 December 1775 to return home without demanding that they sign paroles not to serve until exchanged for British troops. This boded ill for the St. Jean garrison. Since only the 500 prisoners taken at the Cedars were on parole, many of the captured British and Canadians had to wait some time before they could be freed through prisoner exchanges.

Exploration of the West Coast

Trading at Friendly Cove, Nootka Island, in 1788. This picture is also captioned the launching of the North West America, which John Meares had built in Friendly Cove that year.

129

British Columbia is fortunate in not being well-endowed with battle grounds. Her disputes might be said to have been resolved to the south, in Columbia River country. At that, scuffles or skirmishes are more appropriate names for what occurred. Within the province, apart from the sites where fur traders fought each other or parties of natives, and tribe fought tribe, three spots seem to qualify as scenes of conflict, if not actual battlefields. One is the site of Fort Victoria, now obscured by downtown Victoria, where Hudson's Bay company chief factor Roderick Finlayson and his enployees were attacked in 1844 by a few Cowichan Indians. More interesting, and a national historic site that can be visited, is Fort Kitwanga. Here is a native battle ground dating from the early 1800s, before Europeans penetrated the interior of northwestern British Columbia. Kitwanga is located a short drive north of Kitwanga Indian Reserve, where Highway 37 swings north from Highway 16, about midway between the towns of Smithers and Terrace. On a hilltop the Gitwangak people erected cedar dwellings and protected them with a stockade. At Kitwanga village, on the reserve, are totem poles that tell the story of Fort Kitwanga.

The wars against the Gitwangak people by the Haida, Kitimat, Niska and Tsimshian tribes were over food, Gitwangak slaves, and the control of trade routes between the natives of the interior and the coast. Fort Kitwanga was built by a Gitksan war chief named Nekt, who chose a strategic site overlooking the Grease Trail, so-named because of the greasy candlefish oil that was carried along it from the Nass River to the Skeena. Nekt was said to have been killed by the first gun brought into the area. The fort ceased to be a strategic site after 1824 when more natives acquired rifles, and it could be fired on from the Grease Trail. Since 1971, when the mound was acquired by Parks Canada, Fort Kitwanga has been undergoing restoration.

The third battle site is on native land, the Yoquot Reserve at Friendly Cove on Nootka Island. For six years, from 1789 to 1795, that land was in Spanish hands most of the time.

The Nootka Incident 1789-1795 9

European powers became interested in the British Columbia coast in the 1780s, as a source of furs for the China market. Historically, Spain claimed ownership of the entire west coast. In 1778 Captain James Cook explored part of Nootka Sound, and his journals, published in 1784, aroused great interest in the area because of its potential for furs.

Captain James Cook, by N. Dance. Cook's journals, published in 1784, awakened the world to the trading potential of the west coast.

Location of Nootka Island

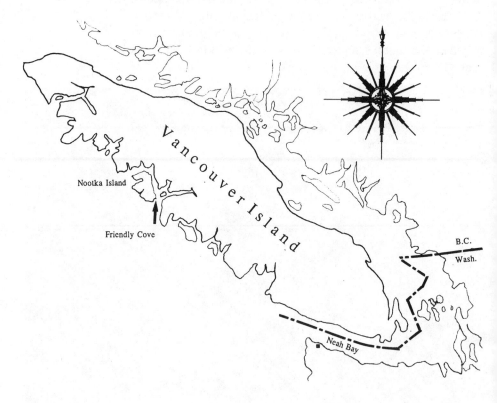

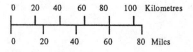

Friendly Cove is on the southeastern tip of Nootka Island and the site overlooks the entrance to Nootka Sound. Neah Bay, where the Spanish set up a trading base, is near the northwestern end of the State of Washington.

Four years later, in 1788, two British ships sailed into Nootka Sound and anchored in Friendly Cove. Both were owned by John Meares, a half-pay lieutenant in the Royal Navy. Meares was in command of the *Felice Aventureira*, while the commander of the other vessel *Efigenia Nubiana*, was William Douglas. The ships bore exotic names because they were sailing under the Portugese flag. They were registered in Macao, Portugal's island colony in China's Canton River. British ships could only trade on the Pacific coast if they held licences from either the East India Company or the South Sea Company. These held the monopoly that extended from Cape Horn westwards to the Cape of Good Hope. But ships under foreign registry were immune from these restrictions.

At Friendly Cove, the Englishmen were met by Muquinna, the local chief of the Nootka Indians. Meares later claimed that Muquinna agreed to sell him an acre of land on the shore of the cove and to grant him a monopoly in the fur trade. Muquinna later declared that he did neither, but he did allow Meares to erect a house with storage work space underneath it. Meares fortified his house with some breastwork, and his crew set to work building a sloop which he named the *North West America*, the first vessel built on the Pacific north coast.

That season two American fur trading ships were in the vicinity – the *Columbia*, Captain John Kendrick, and the *Lady Washington*, Captain Robert Grey. When these ships visited Friendly Cove, Meares was disconcerted to find that he had such competition. In September, Meares' three vessels left Nootka, Meares himself in the *Felice*, bound for Macao. The *Efigenia* and the *North West America* sailed for Hawaii. At Canton during the winter, Meares and others formed a partnership entitled the Associated Merchants Trading to the Northwest Coast of America. Two more trading vessels, the *Princess Royal*, Captain Thomas Hudson, and the *Argonaut*, Captain James Colnett, would join the *Efigenia* and and the *North West America* in the spring of 1789.

Somehow the Spanish in Mexico heard of the British presence at Nootka. In the spring the viceroy of New Spain, Manuel Antonio Florez, dispatched an expedition from San Blas, a Spanish base on the lower Pacific Coast. It consisted of two vessels, the warship *Princesa* and the supply ship *San Carlos*, and it was commanded by Captain Esteban Martinez.   His second-in-command was the master of the *San Carlos*, Captain Gonzales Lopez de Haro. The two Spanish ships were lying off Nootka on 3 May 1789 when the American ship *Lady Washington* appeared. Her commander, Captain Robert Grey, told Martinez of other trading ships in the vicinity and of John Meares' activities in Friendly Cove. Martinez

Muquinna, principal chief at Nootka. John Meares persuaded the chief to let him open his trading post in Friendly Cove.

sailed into the cove and discovered the *Efigenia*. The Spanish officer seized the ship and arrested her captain, William Douglas. Martinez held the ship for a few days; then released it with orders to Douglas to return promptly to Macao.

On 8 June the *North West America* arrived in Friendly Cove, and Martinez seized it, renamed it *Santa Gertrudis la Magna*, and sent it with a Spanish crew to explore. Meanwhile, workmen were constructing two forts, on islands commanding the sound – on San Raphael and on the largest island of the San Miguel group. On 24 June, Martinez took formal possession of Nootka in the name of King Carlos III of Spain.

Then the ships *Princess Royal* and *Argonaut* arrived in the sound on 2 July. The Spaniards noticed the *Princess Royal* first, and launches towed the ship towards the open sea with orders from

Don Estevan José Martinez, commander of several expeditions to the northwest coast, was in charge of the force that evicted the British from Friendly Cove in 1789.

Martinez to Captain Hudson to return to the Orient. Later in the day, Captain James Colnett sailed the *Argonaut* into Friendly Cove bringing twenty-nine Chinese craftsmen and supplies and equipment for founding a permanent settlement. Martinez came aboard the *Argonaut*, arrested Colnett and his crew and took them

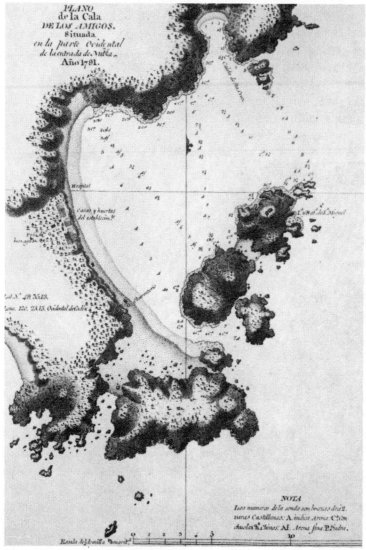

Spanish map of the Cala de los Amigos or Friendly Cove. Shown are the hospital, observatory, houses and gardens, and the well.

ashore. The following day, Martinez raised a Spanish flag on the *Argonaut*, to Colnett's chagrin.

Captain Hudson of the *Princess Royal* had no intention of taking directions from Martinez, and instead of sailing for Macao he continued trading with Indians along the coast. On 12 July he sailed too close to Friendly Cove and Martinez's men captured his ship. The crew and captain were imprisoned aboard because Colnett and

Friendly Cove

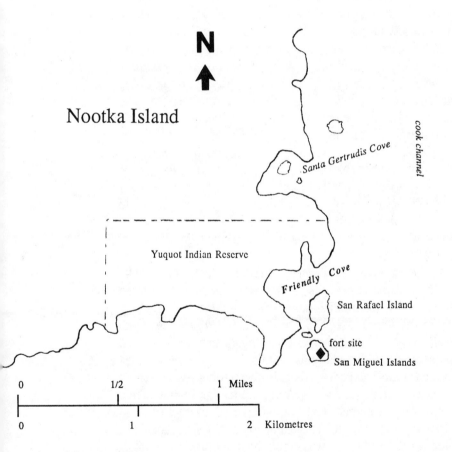

A number of names bestowed by the Spanish are still in use, recalling Spain's interest in the west coast in the 18th century.

the crew of the *Argonaut* were all the Spanish could handle on shore.

The local Indians sympathized with the British, and on the 13th they went in canoes to the *San Carlos* and denounced the actions of the Spanish. Martinez discharged a musket at Callicum, a Nootka chief, missing him. One of the Spanish sailors also fired and his shot killed Callium. Friendly Cove at that point seemed sadly misnamed.

On 14 July the *Argonaut*, manned by a Spanish crew, Captain Colnett and his crew as prisoners, set sail for San Blas. Two weeks later the *Princess Royal* followed, escorted by the *San Carlos*.

The American ships *Columbia* and *Lady Washington* had been in the area all summer, sometimes anchored in Friendly Cove. When these ships were ready to leave for the winter, Martinez sent the crew of the renamed *North West America* on the *Columbia*, which was bound for China. Soon afterwards the supply ship *Aranzazu* arrived from San Blas with orders from the viceroy to evacuate Nootka at the end of the 1789. Someone was having second thoughts about annoying the British.

When news of Martinez's seizure of the four British ships reached London, war loomed. Not feeling in a position to challenge the Royal Navy, Spain signed the Nootka Convention on 28 October 1790. Under its terms Spain agreed to allow British subjects to trade on the Pacific coast, as long as they stayed more than ten leagues away from all Spanish bases. But this was not the end of the matter.

At the close of 1789 a new viceroy, the Condé de Revilla Gigedo, ordered Nootka reoccupied, and he chose Francisco de Eliza to lead a new expedition north. Eliza sailed from San Blas on 3 February 1790 with the ships *Conception*, *San Carlos* and *Princesa Real* (the former *Princess Royal*). He began rebuilding the fort at San Miguel, and garrisoned it with seventy-five Catalonian troops commanded by Don Pedro Alberni. For two years British trading vessels stayed away from Nootka Sound while Britain waited for Spain to abide by the convention signed. In 1792, Spain tried another tactic to retain some control over the Pacific north coast. If Spain could not hold the entire length, she was determined to make the Strait of Juan de Fuca her northern boounbary. Admitting that Nootka might be untenable, the Spanish began a new base at Neah Bay, on what is now the north coast of the State of Washington near Cape Flattery.

Negotiations were to take place at Nootka in the summer, and in preparation, on 29 April, the commander of the Spanish fleet in the Pacific, Juan Francisco de la Bodega y Quadra, arrived in Friendly Cove. British representatives would be coming, and Quadra had a house repaired to be fit to receive visitors. He also established good relations with Muquinna and his people. The chief British negotiator, Captain George Vancouver of the Royal Navy, was already nearby, aboard his ship *Discovery* and escorted by the ship *Chatham*, charting parts of the coastline. On 28 August he brought his ships into Friendly Cove to begin meetings with Quadra.

The negotiations did not go smoothly. Because of British exploration and claims, Vancouver maintained that Britain had a

Monument to Bodega y Quadra. The last Spanish commander at Friendly Cove is commemorated in this statue in Victoria, B.C.

legitimate right to the Columbia River, which conflicted with Spain's determination to have the Strait of Juan de Fuca as her northern boundary. Vancouver had strong objections to the new Spanish base at Neah Bay. Quadra insisted that title to Nootka remain with the Spanish crown, which Vancouver rejected. Next, Quadra claimed that since the site of John Meares' house had been purchased, it could not belong to Britain. Vancouver retorted that Britain would have all of Nootka or he would stop negotiating. Unable to come to any agreements, the two decided to refer the matter to their respective governments for decisions.

All the while, Muquinna displayed a dislike for the British visitors. Quadra acted as a mediator, more than half convinced that Spain would lose Nootka. He felt duty-bound to smooth the way for Muquinna to accept a British presence. Vancouver took his leave, and on 22 September Quadra, too, departed. He left a caretaker garrison in the fort at San Miguel under Lieutenant Salvador Fidalgo. Quadra stopped at Neah Bay and had his workmen demolish the new base to avoid antagonising the British.

Captain George Vancouver again sailed the *Discovery* into Friendly Cove on 2 September 1794, hoping to learn that Britain and Spain had come to an accord over the ownership of Nootka. The Spanish commander was now Jose Manuel de Alava, who had no news. Vancouver agreed to wait until mid-October, and if none came he would return to England. The presence of three Spanish warships and three trading vessels in Friendly Cove did not escape his notice. No word came on an agreement over Nootka, and Vancouver took his leave of Alava. When Vancouver reached England early in 1795 he found that another Nootka Convention had been signed in Madrid on 1 January 1794.

The official transfer occurred on 28 March 1795 at Friendly Cove. The Spanish warship *Activa* brought General Alava from San Blas, and the British representative was Lieutenant Thomas Pearce of the Royal Marines. The British flag was raised and then lowered. After the ceremony, Pearce presented the flag to Muquinna and asked him to raise it whenever a ship appeared.

Under the Nootka Convention, Britain and Spain agreed not to establish any permanent base at Nootka. Ships of both countries could visit the cove, and both agreed to prevent any other power establishing sovereignty. The British and Spanish took away all the

The flag of Spain is shown flying over the fort at the entrance to Nootka Sound.

material that could be moved. The Indians tore down the buildings for the nails they contained and built lodges on the site. All that now remains of the old trading base is the small settlement of Yuquot, along the shore of Friendly Cove, and a marker on the site of the San Miguel Fort.

The War of 1812

An aspect of the war on the Great Lakes. The drawing shows the amphibious landing near Newark (Niagara-on-the-Lake) 1813.

143

The War of 1812 in North America was caused by Britain's preoccupation with France and the Napoleonic Wars. James Madison, the President of the United States, declared war on Britain on 18 June 1812. The main American grievances were over maritime rights — the seizure of British-born naturalized American citizens for service in the Royal Navy; the violations of the United States neutrality and territorial waters; the blockade of American ports; and Britain's refusal to revoke Orders-in-Council made in 1807 which preceded a blockade of European ports to prevent supplies reaching France.

The United States invasions of Upper Canada were not so much annexationist as an attempt to obtain a bargaining tool. If the Americans were in possession of Upper and Lower Canada, Madison thought that he could force Britain to respect American maritime rights. Enthusiasm for the war was strongest in the south and west, among the 'War Hawks' who felt that the American Revolution could not be regarded as complete until Britain had been driven out of North America. To this faction belonged frontiersmen who resented British support for Indians in the Ohio country and along Lake Michigan. To some extent President Madison was caught between the two extremes. Many people in the north and east were displeased with what they called 'Mr. Madison's War'. Since public opinion was divided, the United States war effort was at times half-hearted, which worked to Canada's advantage.

The people of Upper Canada were listless at first. How could Britain's colonies, with a combined population of less than half a million, expel the troops of a nation of eight million? They were reckoning without the courage and drive of their military governor and commander-in-chief in Upper Canada, Major-General Isaac Brock.

In August, the American Brigadier-General William Hull brought an army across the Detroit River and occupied Sandwich (Windsor). Aware that his objective was Amherstburg, Brock left York (Toronto) with some regulars and militia and headed in Hull's direction. On hearing that Brock was on his way, Hull withdrew to Detroit. When Brock reached Amherstburg, the troops he brought with him augmented those of the local garrison commander, Major-General Henry Procter. Brock was able to form a field force of 300 regulars and 400 militiamen. He joined forces

Setting for Queenston Heights

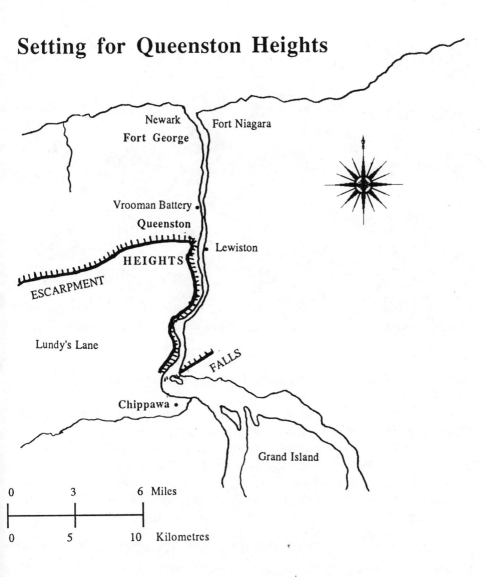

The heights where the battle was fought lie on top of the Niagara escarpment that is such a prominent local feature. South of the heights the escarpment forms the Niagara gorge, beyond which lie the falls.

with the Shawnee warrior Tecumseh, who had brought 600 braves, and they crossed the Detroit River. On 16 August Hull surrendered 1,600 militiamen and nearly 600 American regulars to Brock. This dashing move, aided immeasurably by the terror Tecumseh's painted followers invoked, won over the confidence of

Scene from the Battle of Moraviantown, in the Thames valley, where the Shawnee war leader, Tecumseh, was killed on 6 October 1813.

the Upper Canadians. With a leader like Brock, anything seemed possible.

Brock needed their confidence, for he had to have their cooperation. His force of regulars in Upper Canada numbered scarcely 1,200 — the 41st and 49th Regiments and some Royal Artillery. To supplement his meagre force of professionals, he formed flank companies as part of each militia regiment. These companies received more training than the rest of the militia force, so that they could serve as rallying points for their regiments, or operate with regulars. After his success at Detroit, Brock returned to his main headquarters, at Fort George, outside the town of Newark (Niagara-on-the-Lake). An attack across the Niagara River was more than likely.

Major-General Isaac Brock was a native of Guernsey, who attained the rank of lieutenant-colonel of the 49th Regiment of Foot in 1797, at age twenty-eight. The 49th had been in Canada since 1802, and Brock had come with it, but he had made trips back to England from time to time. In 1810, he was appointed adminstrator of the government of Upper Canada, and commander-in-chief. He was distressed that he was stuck in Canada while many of his

146

brother officers were winning battle honours in Europe, serving under the Duke of Wellington. His capable subordinate in command on the Niagara frontier was Major-General Roger Sheaffe, like Brock a career soldier, but one who was more cautious. Brock's *aide-de-camp* was Lieutenant-Colonel John Macdonell, from Glengarry County.

Today, the site of the Battle of Queenston Heights is a large, land-scaped area maintained as part of the Niagara Parks Commission's system along the Niagara River. The setting is spectacular, on the brow of the Niagara Escarpment above the Niagara Gorge and over-looking Queenston, which lies at the base of the escarpment. The spray from the great falls rises not far to the south. Brock's Monument, where he and his *aide-de-camp* Macdonell are buried, crowns the site, and the monument is maintained by Parks Canada. The spot where Brock is thought to have fallen is marked by a tablet that was unveiled in 1860 by the then Prince of Wales, later King Edward VII.

Before the October battle, troops stationed along the Niagara River were detachments of the 41st and 49th Regiments of Foot, resplendent in red coats, and most of the Lincoln County militia, a few in the green coats of citizen-soldiers, others in red or civilian dress. Also present were part of the York militia from the capital,

View of the American garrison at old Fort Niagara from Upper Canada in 1806. The pen and ink drawing was made by Sempronius Stretton.

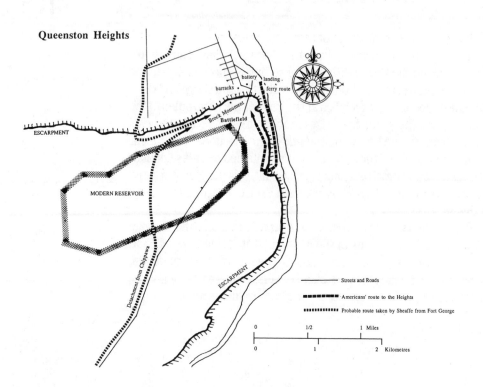

Queenston Heights

battery
landing
barracks
ferry route
Brock Monument
Battlefield
ESCARPMENT
MODERN RESERVOIR
Detachment from Chippawa
ESCARPMENT

———————— Streets and Roads

■■■■■■■■ Americans' route to the Heights

ııııııııı Probable route taken by Sheaffe from Fort George

| 0 | 1/2 | 1 Miles |

| 0 | 1 | 2 Kilometres |

Detail of the battle. A modern reservoir stands on part of the site.

and detachments of regular and militia artillery. Across the Niagara River, American troops were massing under the command of Major-General Stephen Van Rensselaer. He had little experience as a military commander, but he was a successful politician.

As the October days passed, Brock sought information on Van Rensselaer's plans. He suspected that the activity across the Niagara River, in the vicinity of Lewiston, was a feint, and the real attack would be against Fort George. On his part, Van Rensselaer was convinced that Brock planned to attack him. The American commander had 900 regulars and 2,650 militia at Lewiston. All told, 6,000 American troops were gathered along the river, and this number included 1,650 other regulars under Brigadier-General Alexander Smyth, a regular officer who wanted nothing to do with Van Rensselaer. In the British army, a regular officer was never subordinate to a militia officer. In the American army, militia officers of higher rank could command regular officers.

Brock's main body of troops was at Fort George, but he had detachments of troops at Fort Erie and Chippawa to guard the crossings above Niagara Falls, which were easier to penetrate than those below the great cascade. At Queenston he had posted a 3-pounder gun and the grenadier company of the 49th Regiment. An 18-pounder had been placed in a small redan halfway upslope above Queenston — but not high enough for its outline to be visible from the American shore. The gun was manned by some artillerymen, and the light company of the 49th was stationed there. A 24-pounder had been placed at Vrooman's Point, not quite two kilometres down stream from Queenston.

Van Rensselaer decided that he would launch his attack on the heights above Queenston. At 3.00 a.m. on 13 October, under artillery bombardment from the American shore, he sent out thirteen boats carrying 300 volunteers under the command of his cousin, Colonel Solomon Van Rensselaer. The Americans were pinned down by fire from the grenadiers of the 49th once they were ashore, but Captain John Wool of the 13th United States Infantry led his company up the path that led to the heights.

Back in Fort George, Brock was aroused by the noise of the American artillery. Once he knew for certain that the affair at the heights was no feint, he ordered flank companies of the York militia forward, left orders for Sheaffe to bring the Fort George garrison, and galloped for the redan on the slope above Queenston. He ordered the light company of the 49th to Queenston to support the hard-pressed grenadier company. At the redan the gunners were firing round shot at the boats carrying more Americans to the Canadian shore. Then Brock spotted Captain John Wool and his American regulars coming over the crest of the heights. With a mighty yell they ran downslope towards the redan. The gunners spiked the 18-pounder and fled, Brock running beside them leading his horse. Brock came close to being captured or killed before they reached Queenston.

Now he became even more rash. He determined to retake the redan at once, before the Americans could control the commanding position on the heights. At the head of 100 of the 49th and 100 wavering Lincoln militia, he led the charge up the hill towards Wool's men — a conspicuous figure with his gold lace and accoutrements that marked him as a high-ranking officer. A shot through his wrist did not stop him, but a marksman shot him through the chest, and he fell, mortally wounded.

At that moment aide-de-camp Lieutenant-Colonel John Macdonell, arrived leading two flank companies of the York militia (and the legend of the dying Brock calling 'Push on York volunteers' was born). Macdonell launched a second attack and recaptured the redan. The Americans, too, had been reinforced from Queenston. In the firing that followed, Macdonell was also mortally wounded, and the leaderless regulars and militia retired downhill and towards Vrooman's Point to await reinforcements. Captain Wool had been wounded, and Lieutenant-Colonel Winfield Scott, a twenty-six-year-old Virginian, arrived to take over. Then Van Rensselaer crossed the river and ordered Brigadier-General William Wadsworth of the militia to assume command. Van Rensselaer soon returned to the New York side of the river.

There, most of the New York militiamen were refusing to cross into Canada. Militiamen were not required to serve outside the United States and no amount of cajoling could make some of them budge. They were also intimidated by the accuracy of the fire against their boats. Some of the 1,300 men who had crossed over managed to return. Only 350 regulars and 250 militia were holding the heights, and their ammunition was running low. The rest of the American invaders were at Queenston. In the background, the guns of Fort George and Fort Niagara traded shots, adding to the din.

At noon, Major-General Sheaffe reached Vrooman's Point with some horse-drawn artillery, 300 all ranks of the 41st Regiment, and 250 militia — the Niagara Light Dragoons, Captain Robert Runchey's company of blacks from St. Catharines, and the flank companies of the Lincoln militia. He was soon joined by the grenadier company of the 41st Regiment from Chippawa and more militia, which brought his force to 400 regulars and the same number of militia. A force of about 100 Indians from their lands along the Grand River had reached the scene ahead of Sheaffe, and he sent them ahead as skirmishers. Their leader was John Norton (Teyoninhokarawen).

Sheaffe decided not to try a frontal assault from the river. Instead he led his force by a circuitous route and up the slope from the west,

152

The old 'French Castle' inside Fort Niagara. The fort, built by the French and occupied by the British until 1796, had a garrison of American troops during the War of 1812-1814.

extending into line of battle as he approached. The Americans were taken by surprise, and they had no time to throw up any breastworks, although they had been digging in on the Queenston side in anticipation of an attack from the river road. Sheaffe's men fired one volley, then fixed bayonets for a charge. The Americans fired raggedly and fled downhill towards Queenston. Some, terrorized by the sight of the Indians whose strength had now risen to 300 warriors, found places to hide and remained concealed until Winfield Scott was seen waving something white.

The report prepared by Brigade-Major Thomas Evans showed that 1 brigadier-general (Wadsworth), 1 major aide-de-camp, 5 lieutenant-colonels, 3 majors, 19 captains, 32 lieutenants, 10 ensigns, 1 adjutant, 1 surgeon, 852 non-commissioned officers and privates — a total of 925 — were prisoners of war. Of these, 19 officers and 417 other ranks were regulars; 54 officers and 435 other ranks were militia. Evans estimated American casualties at 500 in killed and wounded. Many of the latter had been removed to the American side. Included on a list of captured equipment was one 6-pounder gun, which was probably not used.

Evans' return of British casualties read:

General Staff — 2 killed (Brock and Macdonell)

Royal Artillery — 2 rank and file wounded

Detachment 41st Regiment — 1 sergeant, 1 rank and file killed; 1 sergeant, 9 rank and file wounded.

John Brant, son of the Mohawk war chief Joseph Brant. John was with the Six Nations warriors who came from their lands on the Grand River to reinforce the troops at Queenston Heights.

Flank companies 49th Regiment — 8 rank and file killed; 2 captains, 3 sergeants, 27 rank and file, 1 volunteer wounded; 5 rank and file, 1 volunteer missing.

Lincoln Artillery — 1 rank and file wounded.

Lincoln Militia — 1 adjutant, 1 sergeant, 13 rank and file wounded; 10 rank file missing.

York Militia — 2 rank and file killed; 1 lieutenant, 1 sergeant, 15 rank and file wounded, 5 rank and file missing.

Thus 14 regulars and 2 militia were killed, 33 regulars and 32 militia wounded, and 1 regular and 15 militia were missing at the end of the battle. Indian casualties were 9 wounded and 5 killed.

Van Rensselaer sent a message to Scheaffe asking for a three day armistice. Sheaffe agreed because he had more prisoners to cope with than troops. He allowed the militia to go home and sent only the 489 American regulars to Quebec City as prisoners-of-war.

The wounded, both American and British and Canadian, were carried to Newark. Many were cared for in St. Mark's Church and the Indian Council House. Brock and Macdonell were interred temporarily on 16 October in the northeast or cavalier bastion of Fort George also known as the York Battery. When the first Brock Monument had been erected in 1824 the bodies of Brock and Mac-

The Battle of Queenston Heights. Queenston village is on the right with the heights above it. American troops are shown crossing from Lewiston, N.Y.

Battle of Lundy's Lane. One of the bloodiest encounters, it was fought on 25 July 1814 and ended when the Americans withdrew to Fort Erie.

donell were moved there. When the monument was damaged by a bomb in 1840, the bodies were removed to the Hamilton family cemetery, and re-interred on completion of the second monument. Brock was made a Knight of the Bath on 9 October, for his victory at Detroit, news that did not reach him before his death at Queenston Heights. Sheaffe was created a baronet for his success after Brock fell.

Queenston Heights was one of the early battles of the War of 1812, but through its success, and that at Detroit two months before, the morale of the Canadians was greatly improved. In fact, the Americans, who had every advantage, frittered their resources through indecision and errors, and never did regain the momentum necessary for a successful campaign. The American system of allowing militia officers to be senior to regulars had serious defects. By the end of 1812, the Canadians knew that even when outnumbered they could win. The militia showed considerable competence, but the steadiness of the British regulars was nearly always a factor in repulsing the enemy.

The Battle of Stoney Creek June 1813

11

Stoney Creek was one of a series of major and minor encounters that took place on the Niagara Peninsula in 1813. The battle was a minor one, but it had an impact on the conduct of the Americans afterwards. Much has been made of the site. Part of the ground has been preserved as Battlefield Park in the centre of Stoney Creek. Battlefield House, in the park, is a museum. At the time of the battle it belonged to James and Mary Gage, prominent local residents. The park is on the south side of King Street. Across from it on the north is a small lion monument to those who fell. A monument commemorating the battle is inside the park. Each year, people in period dress re-enact the battle, using the correct drill and formations of 1813.

The United States campaign of 1813 in this locality began in late May, when an American army of 7,000 men and a naval squadron began a combined operation against Fort George, at the town of Newark (Niagara-on-the-Lake). In command of the American fleet was Commodore Isaac Chauncey, and the land force was under Major-General Henry Dearborn, a veteran of the American Revolution and past his prime. When Dearborn's army attacked Fort George, the British defenders — 1,400 men under Major-General John Vincent — were soon forced to evacuate their position.

A modern view of Battlefield House, Stoney Creek from the front. At the time of the battle, the house was the property of the Gage family.

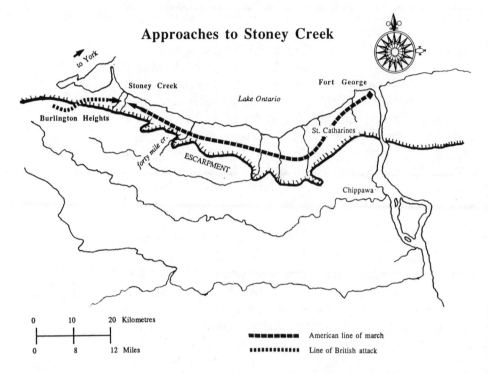

Approaches to Stoney Creek

to York

Stoney Creek

Fort George

Lake Ontario

Burlington Heights

St. Catharines

forty mile cr.

ESCARPMENT

Chippawa

| 0 | 10 | 20 Kilometres |
| 0 | 8 | 12 Miles |

■■■■■■■■ American line of march

ııııııııııı Line of British attack

The Americans marched from Fort George, pausing at Forty Mile Creek. The British, who had retreated to Burlington Heights, descended on the American bivouac at Stoney Creek under cover of darkness.

Vincent's expelled garrison was some companies of the 8th (King's) Regiment, a detachment of the 41st, and the whole of the 49th — the late General Isaac Brock's unit now commanded by Vincent — some Royal Newfoundland Fencibles and Glengarry Light Infantry Fencibles, and 300 militiamen from flank companies. In the battle, before he resolved to withdraw, Vincent lost 52 killed and 306 wounded or missing.

With the survivors, Vincent marched across country, parallel to the Niagara River and then in the direction of Beaver Dam, where he had a supply depot. There he was joined by two more companies of the 8th Regiment that had been driven from Fort Erie by the Americans, and a naval party from Amherstburg. With a force that now amounted to 1,600 regulars and fencibles, Vincent dismissed his militiamen and allowed them to return to their homes. He continued on to Burlington Heights, on the top of the escarp-

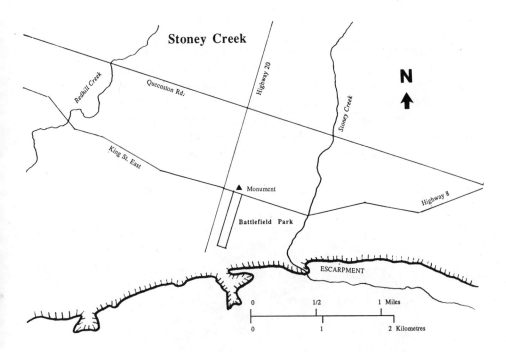

Battlefield Park, on the south side of Highway 2 (King Street) covers a small part of the actual battle site.

ment above Burlington Bay. From there he could be supplied by the British fleet commanded by Captain Sir James Yeo that was based at Kingston. With the Americans holding Fort Erie and Fort George, Vincent's supply line along the Niagara River had been severed.

At Fort George, Major-General Winfield Scott was in command, because Dearborn was ill. Scott ordered a pursuit force to move westwards and find a spot from which to prevent Vincent linking up with Major-General Henry Proctor, then occupying Detroit. Scott assigned 3,000 infantrymen, 150 cavalry and 4 field guns, under two brigadier-generals, William Winder and John Chandler, for the expedition to confine Vincent. Brigadiers Winder and Chandler set out from Fort George in pursuit of Vincent's troops on the 4th and camped that night at Forty Mile Creek. On 3 June, Sir James Yeo, in command of the Royal Navy and Provincial Marine vessels, left Kingston with a squadron bound for Niagara carrying supplies and 300 fresh troops from the 8th Regiment. Yeo's mission had a bearing on the actions of the American officers after the battle at Stoney Creek.

On the 5th the Americans marched on to the neighbourhood of Stoney Creek, a small settlement named after the branches of the stream that flowed down the face of the Niagara Escarpment, meandered across the flat and emptied into the Lake Ontario. The American camp was poorly organised, with each commander deciding where his men would bivouac. No attempt was made to place the centre, left and right wings in spots where they could form a battle line quickly. Few sentries were posted. The American camp was about ten kilometres from that of Vincent's army on

Captain Sir James Yeo, Royal Navy. Yeo was the commander of the Royal Navy and Provincial Marine squadrons on Lake Ontario in 1813.

Burlington Heights.

Vincent's second-in-command, Lieutenant-Colonel John Harvey, a Deputy Adjutant-General in Canada, led a party to reconnoitre the American camp, and when they returned Harvey recommended that Vincent organise a night attack. The night was dark for that time of the year, and Vincent agreed to proceed. A spy had visited him and gave him the American countersign. Vincent chose 700 men, from the 8th and 49th Regiments. Major Charles Plenderleath would have the field command of the 49th. Lieutenant-Colonel Harvey commanded the attack and Major James Ogilvie of the 49th led the men of the 8th. Vincent set out, and his force reached the American camp at 2.00 a.m. on 6 June, incidently the birthday of King George III. With bayonets fixed the regulars ran, whooping like Indians, down upon what they thought was the American camp, but they found only dying fires and a few cooks. The enemy had moved to higher ground for the night, with orders to sleep on their arms. The element of surprise was lost.

While the British paused to load their muskets, they were in full view of the Americans, who had time to rally somewhat, and several of the regulars were killed. The 49th, about 500 strong, wheeled to the left while the 8th moved to the right. Before the

The back of Battlefield House facing the gardens. The house is now the museum for the battle site.

49th could form a line the Americans sent out a barrage of fire. The British could not hear their officers' commands, and they began to fall back. At this crucial moment Major Plenderleath, with about twenty men of the 49th, dashed up the road and into the face of four of the American guns that were mounted on Smith's knoll (where the lion monument now stands). The Americans managed to fire two volleys before Plenderleath and his men were upon them and capturing their four artillery pieces. The men of the 49th turned the guns on their former owners, while everywhere confusion ruled. Here was an occasion when the well-trained and usually steady British regulars got out of hand.

Lieutenant James FitzGibbon of the 49th lamented that the regulars had become so excited by the uncertainties of a night attack that they were less effective than they ought to have been. (He remembered the confusion of Stoney Creek on a December night in 1837 when he sent a picket against Mackenzie's rebels, who fled after being fired upon in the dark). The reports of both

Re-enactment of the Battle of Stoney Creek. Volunteers in the uniforms of the 49th and 41st Regiments, 1812-1814, stage the battle each year in Battlefield Park.

the British Harvey and the American Chandler attested to the disorder that prevailed at Stoney Creek. Many officers did not know who was who. Chandler was wounded, trying to rally some troops he encountered. They were from the 49th Regiment and Chandler found himself a prisoner. Winder was also captured, and the command of the American troops fell upon Colonel James Burn of the 2nd Light Dragoons. Burn held a meeting with such officers as he could find, who reported that they were short of ammunition. Burn ordered a withdrawal back to Forty Mile Creek. From there the army could be supplied for another movement against Vincent, or if General Scott had other ideas, await his orders. Major-General Vincent, too, was almost captured. He got lost and after wandering about he found his way back to Burlington Heights on the morning of 7 June.

Because of the conditions under which the battle was fought, Vincent, the victor, lost more men than Chandler and Winder — 214 killed, wounded and missing as against 168 American losses. Vincent's attack might have been total a failure had the Americans not been deprived of their two brigadiers. Chandler and Winder might have rallied them as daylight came on and they became aware of their numerical superiority.

The American force, now led by Colonel Burn, camped the night of 6 June at Forty Mile Creek, but not for long. On the 7th, Sir James Yeo's squadron appeared offshore, and he sent in two warships to bombard the American camp. Burn ordered his men to decamp and march for Fort George. Yeo's squadron had intercepted sixteen boatloads of supplies that Scott had dispatched for the relief of Burn's men. By the 8th, Burn and his force were back at Fort George.

After the defeat at Stoney Creek the Americans felt so demoralised that they withdrew from all the positions they had been holding on the Niagara Peninsula except Fort George. They built new earthworks and brought every available boat to the Canadian side of the Niagara River, to ensure that if they were pressed too hard, they would be able to retire to Fort Niagara, on the New York side of the river.

Beaver Dam, the battle that gave Canadians an enduring national heroine in Laura Secord, was fought on 24 June. Lieutenant James FitzGibbon, warned by Laura and also by Indian scouts, defeated a punitive force sent from Fort George to capture the supply depot. FitzGibbon had fifty regulars at Beaver Dam, but the fighting was for the most part done by 400 Indians. Some 460 Americans surrendered to FitzGibbon because he offered them protection from the scalping knife.

The Americans soon abandoned Fort Erie, which the British reoccupied. Then in December the American garrison left Fort George, burned the town of Newark, and retired to Fort Niagara on their own territory. Another season of campaigning on the Niagara frontier still remained before the war was ended. But to the east, the highlights of the 1813 season — the decisive Battles of Chateauguay and Crysler's Farm — dealt a fatal blow to American hopes for the capture of Montreal.

The Stoney Creek Battle Monument. This memorial stands in Battlefield Park. A second monument in the form of a lion stands north of the park and commemorates the men who fell in the battle.

The Battle of Chateauguay
October 1813

12

In the autumn of 1813, during the second year of the War of 1812, the Americans inflicted heavy losses on the Canadian and British forces, but they were foiled in an attempt to capture Montreal. A two pronged attack was planned. One American army under Major-General Wade Hampton approached from New York State along the Chateauguay River. Hampton's force numbered about 4,000 men and was to proceed overland from New York state. The second army, 8,000 strong, and commanded by Major-General James Wilkinson, formed at Sackets Harbor and moved in boats down the St. Lawrence. Hampton's army, poorly equipped and clad, turned back after the Battle of Chateauguay.

The Crysler's farm battle ground was flooded during construction of the St. Lawrence Seaway, and the present Crysler Battlefield Park does not resemble the original site. The site of the Chateauguay battle, however, is upstream from Allans Corners and is a national historic park. The park is small, and it does not cover the whole of the battle ground, which stretched out from Ormstown to a spot some two kilometres downstream from Allans Corners.

Unlike most of the other battles of the War of 1812, Chateauguay was fought entirely by Canadians and Indians, without the backing of British regulars. The man who commanded the battle was both – a Canadian who was a professional British officer – Charles d'Irumberry de Salaberry. His father was the Seigneur of Beauport, near Quebec City, and the de Salaberrys mixed freely with the British elite stationed in Canada. Among the family friends was the Duke of Kent, Queen Victoria's father, who had been stationed in Canada in the 1790s. The young Charles went to England and was commissioned in the 60th Regiment, rising to the rank of major in the 5th battalion under the command of Major-General Baron Francis de Rottenburg. After serving in the Napoleonic Wars, de Salaberry returned to Canada in April 1810. He came as an aide-de-camp to de Rottenburg, who had been appointed to the staff of the governor, Lieutenant-General Sir George Prevost.

With war clouds on the horizon, Prevost had to look to his militia to reinforce his meagre garrison of British regulars. Aware of Prevost's dilemma, de Salaberry proposed that he raise a militia regiment to be called the Canadian Voltigeurs. Prevost, who harboured a dislike of de Salaberry formed while both men were serving in England, grudgingly accepted the offer. The War Office

Setting for Chateauguay Battle

de Salaberry

(Allans Co

(Monumen

breastworks

abatis

swampy woods

Hampton

American Camp at Spears

(Ormstown)

main road

Purdy

Chateauguay River

swampy woods

De Salaberry chose a position along the ravine that extends from Brysonville, on the east side of the Chateauguay River, across the river and westwards. Hampton's main force approached along the main road on the west bank of the Chateauguay.

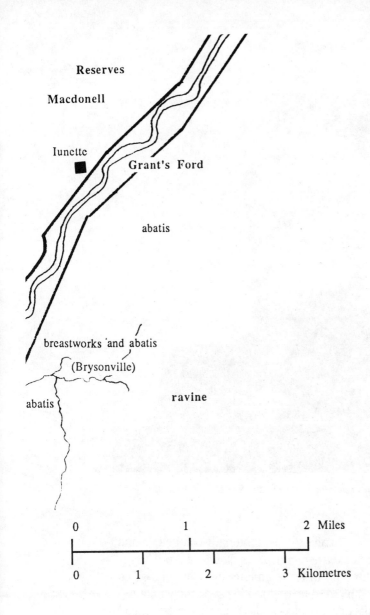

Reserves

Macdonell

Iunette

Grant's Ford

abatis

breastworks and abatis

(Brysonville)

abatis

ravine

| 0 | | 1 | | 2 | Miles |

| 0 | 1 | 2 | 3 | Kilometres |

Charles de Salaberry, the commander of the Canadian troops at the Battle of Chateauguay.

order, awarding de Salaberry a lieutenant-colonelcy and empowering him to raise the regiment, is dated 12 April 1812. Prevost set about forming other regiments of select embodied militia for full-time duty, and he ordered his sedentary militia – which was composed of every able-bodied man between sixteen and sixty – to hold themselves ready to be embodied when required.

De Salaberry's second-in-command was Lieutenant-Colonel 'Red George' Macdonell, then the commander of the 1st Light Regiment of Select Embodied Militia that was composed of flank companies of several regiments. Macdonell and his regiment had been stationed at Kingston when they were ordered to Chateauguay on 21 October. With his regiment he had endured a difficult journey in open boats down the rapids of the St. Lawrence. He had already had some success against the Americans, for he had defeated them at Ogdensburg, New York, that February.

General Hampton had tried to enter Lower Canada in September by way of the Richelieu River, but he turned back near Odelltown, mainly because the summer had been very dry and the stream levels were so low that he could not find enough water for his men and horses. He then moved to Chateauguay Four Corners, on the upper reaches of the Chateauguay River inside New York State and set up camp. On receiving orders from his superior, Lieutenant-General John Armstrong, to effect a junction with Wilkinson at the mouth of the Chateauguay, Hampton left camp with 4,000 troops on 19 October, taking some supply wagons and artillery. His second-in-command was Brigadier-General George Izard, a capable field officer. The main route lay along the north bank of the Chateauguay River. The army was not in high spirits. Hampton had not been able to move many supplies from his depot at Plattsburg, and his men were in their worn-out summer uniforms. He received orders to go into winter camp after he set out, but he could not act on them. His vanguard, under Colonel Robert Purdy, was too far ahead to be called back. Furthermore, Hampton's sources of intelligence were faulty, and he did not know the size of forces that might oppose him.

Hampton's first objective was Spears (Ormstown) where a Canadian picket was stationed. Hampton detailed Izard to lead some light troops in a flanking movement to capture the picket. Izard succeeded, but most of the Canadians eluded him and hurried to inform de Salaberry the location of Hampton's force. On his part, Hampton knew that he was coming close to de Salaberry's lines and he made camp. The Americans marched north in de Salaberry's direction on 22 October. Some ten kilometres separated the two armies, but Hampton's progress was slow. Canadians had felled trees to impede the Americans, and Hampton had to stop frequently while his men removed the trees and repaired the road.

De Salaberry had been watching Hampton since he crossed the border to Odelltown in September. Informers told him that Hampton would move along the Chateauguay River to meet Wilkinson, and de Salaberry moved his Voltigeurs and select embodied and sedentary militia to the Chateauguay and set up a

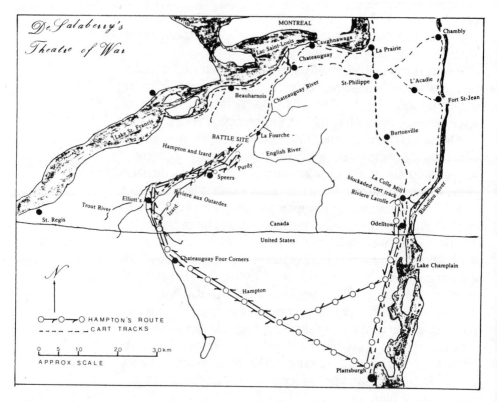

De Salaberry's Theatre of War

MONTREAL

Chambly

Caughnawaga

Chateauguay

La Prairie

Lac Saint-Louis

Beauharnois

Chateauguay River

St-Philippe

L'Acadie

Fort St-Jean

Lake St. Francis

BATTLE SITE

La Fourche –

Hampton and Izard

English River

Burtonville

Purdy

Speers

La Colle Mill

blockaded cart track

Elliott's

Riviere aux Outardes

Riviere Lacolle

Trout River

Izard

Richelieu River

St. Regis

Canada

Odelltown

United States

Chateauguay Four Corners

Lake Champlain

Hampton

○ ─▸○─▸ ○ HAMPTON'S ROUTE
─ ─ ─ ─ ─ CART TRACKS

0   5   10   20   30 km
APPROX. SCALE

Plattsburgh

American General Wade Hampton's movements in October 1813.

headquarters at Sainte Martine. He also picked the spot where he would confront Hampton.

At a bend in the river was a ravine (west of Brysonville) that ran at right angles to the main road, where some cleared land made a satisfactory field of fire. There, on the northern edge of the ravine, he established a line of breastworks on each side of the river, with the stronger line on the west side. The site was also protected by a large swampy wood to the south, where Indians and a few buglers – for extra noise to suggest a large force – would be placed. When the Americans drew near, these breastworks of logs with abatis in front would be occupied by the light company of the Canadian Fencibles under Captain George Ferguson, two companies of Voltigeurs led by Captains Jean-Baptiste and Michel-Louis Juchereau Duchesnay, some Indians under Captain Joseph

Canadian Voltigeurs on picket duty, a miserable assignment.

Lamothe, and a company of Beauharnois militia under Captain Joseph-Marie Longuetin. On the opposite side of the ravine, a small breastwork and abatis would serve as a vantage point to watch for Hampton's vanguard.

At the breastwork on the south (east) side of the river he placed one company of Macdonell's Select Embodied Militia under Captain Charles Daly, a company of *chasseurs* led by Joseph-Bernard Bruyère, and another company of Select Embodied Militia commanded by Captain de Tonnancour.

About two kilometres downstream was Grant's Ford, and this line on the south bank of the river would intercept American troops attempting a flanking movement to reach the ford and thus to cut off de Salaberry's front line from his reserves. As a further measure, de Salaberry had his men build a lunette, a large two-sided log fortification.

Some 300-350 men were in these two front lines, one on either side of the river. Behind were the reserves numbering 1,400 and commanded by Red George Macdonell. The men had built barricades at intervals of from 200 to 300 metres. Behind the first barricade were Captains Benjamin I'Ecuyer and Dominique Debartzch (the seigneur whose home was later taken over for a rebel headquarters at St. Charles in 1837). Behind these were reserves from the 2nd battalion of embodied militia under Captain Jean Baptiste Hertel de Rouville. Protecting the right flank, in some woods, were sedentary militia from Boucherville and Beauharnois under Lieutenant-Colonel Louis René Chaussegros de Léry. Militia under Captain Philippe Panet guarded the ford over the river.

On Monday 25 October, scouts informed Hampton that only 350 Canadians manned de Salaberry's front line on the main road. Hampton chose Colonel Robert Purdy to lead a flanking operation to march on Grant's ford from the south shore, with a force of 1,500 from the 4th, 32nd, and 34th regiments of American infantry. Once Purdy had reached the ford and was ready to cut off de Salaberry's front line from his reserves, he was to attack and when Hampton heard the shooting he would order Brigadier Izard to lead the frontal assault. The guides assigned to lead Purdy's force complained that they did not know the way, but Hampton saw no alternative and trusted to luck. Purdy left on the night of the 25th, but his men did not make good time. Their guides led them, deliberately or not, through a hemlock swamp. In fact, they never did reach the ford; when they found the river bank they were far short of the ford, and in front of de Salaberry's line on the south side of the river.

On the morning of the 26th, Hampton began his advance towards de Salaberry's line on the north shore of the river, but he stopped and waited out of range for the shots from Purdy's men that would tell him that his subordinate was in position. When Hampton did hear firing, Purdy was not at the ford, but exchanging shots with Captain Bruyère's *chasseurs* armed with rifles. The time was perhaps 2.00 p.m. when Hampton went into action.

Some versions suggest that de Salaberry started the battle and fired the first shot. When an American officer who knew some French called on the Canadians to surrender, de Salaberry shot him, and the cheer that rose from the front lines resounded as the reserves took it up. Bugles sounding from the woods to the south, and from all the lines, added to the din. The shooting continued for hours, the front line on the main road holding its own, while the front line on the south bank was contending with Purdy's confused force. Some time after 4.00 p.m. Hampton realized that Purdy was being battered and had no hope of reaching the ford to outflank de Salaberry, and disheartened, he ordered a withdrawal. De Salaberry had stood on a stump throughout the battle, and he later wrote to his father that at the battle he rode a wooden horse.

North of the battle ground, Sir George Prevost and Major-General

Sir George Prevost, commander-in-chief in the Canadas during the War of 1812-1814.

Louis de Watteville were nearly at the line, with escorts but no rein-forcements. Fortunately, de Salaberry would not need help, although he did not know that at the time. He fully expected Hampton to regroup and try again, and he kept his barricades manned and sent a force to pursue the Americans. However, Hampton had had enough.

Purdy led the rearguard, taking up a position beyond the bend in the road. Gradually he fell back, and pursuing troops found abandoned equipment strewn along the road. Indians following and lurking in the woods further unnerved the soldiers shivering in their inadequate clothing.

De Salaberry's casualties were light. Four Select Embodied Militia were killed and four wounded, and three Voltigeurs had been wounded. Hampton estimated that fifty of his men had been killed, but his losses could have been higher. The Canadians buried forty American dead and the Americans buried some of their own. Thus ended the battle that may well have saved Montreal in October 1813.

The number of de Salaberry's men that were engaged was about 300, and all were in the front line of breastworks. The reserves were used briefly, to reinforce Captain Daly on the south bank of the Chateauguay when Purdy's force arrived, and after the battle in pursuit of Hampton's army towards Spears, now Ormstown.

On 11 November, the other army making for Montreal met with disaster. Major-General James Wilkinson's force that had been descending the St. Lawrence River was pursued by a smaller one under Lieutenant-Colonel Joseph Morrison. Wilkinson's rearguard was soundly defeated at Crysler's farm near Morrisburg. When he received word that Hampton would not be on hand for a joint-assualt on Montreal, Wilkinson gave up the attempt and took his men to winter quarters. Thus, if de Salaberry had not won at Chateauguay, and Hampton and Wilkinson had captured Montreal, the course of the war would have been very different. Perhaps the Americans would have succeeded in conquering Canada at a time when Britain, busy fighting Napoleon, could not spare many troops for a Canadian defence.

The War continued for another year. One of the most bitterly con-tested battles was fought at Lundy's Lane in the Niagara Peninsula on 25-26 August 1814, but the outcome was indecisive. As time

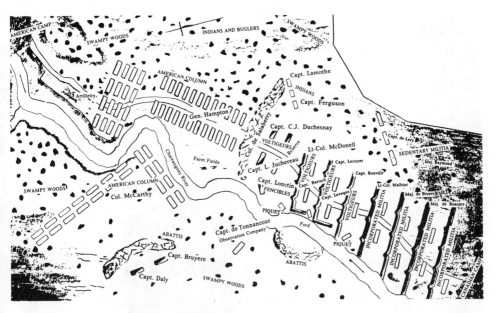

The battle plan of Chateauguay as de Salaberry reported it shortly after the battle.

Obelisk close to the site of the Battle of Chateauguay. Similar obelisks were erected at other 1812 battle sites.

De Salaberry's gravestone. This marker may be seen in the churchyard at Chambly, Quebec.

passed, the issue that had sparked the United States declaration of war evaporated. With the first defeat of Napoleon, Britain no longer felt the need to press men for service in the Royal Navy. Thus the United States could no longer complain that British ships were seizing American citizens of British birth. By 1814 part of Wellington's army was not needed in Europe, although the Battle of Waterloo had yet to be fought, and British regulars were reinforcing the Canadas in large numbers.

The Treaty of Ghent was signed on 24 December 1814, ending the war. By its terms, all captured territories were to be returned. Yet one bit of territory – Carleton Island – was not returned to Britain. Fort Haldimand, on the island, at the head of the St. Lawrence River, had a small caretaker garrison in 1812. A boatload of Americans rowed out from Millen's Bay and seized the fort and declared Carleton Island part of New York State, and so it remains.

Ruins of Fort Haldimand, Carleton island, after 1812. The island was the only territorial change resulting from the war. Until June 1812, it had a British garrison. The Americans seized the island and retained it.

Rebellions in the Canadas

Colonel George Wetherall's troops passing the Richelieu River by night. From a sketch by Lord Charles Beauclerk of the 1st Royals, lithographed by N. Hartnell.

Political and other grievances led to the rebellions of 1837. Two risings occurred in Upper Canada – Mackenzie's on Yonge Street north of Toronto, and Duncombe's assembly of rebels at Scotland, near Brantford. Both were minor affairs that drew very little public support. The outbreaks in Lower Canada were much more serious, and complicated by tensions between the English-speaking minority and the French-speaking majority. Mackenzie's rebels were for the most part farmers and labourers, but many who supported the Lower Canadian *Patriote* leader, Louis-Joseph Papineau, were intellectuals, well-educated and with enough money to live well.

St. Charles, Quebec (Lower Canada), November 1837

13

The site of the Battle of St. Charles is in an area that has not changed as much as the places where other battles of 1837-1838 were fought. Located on the east side of the Richelieu River half way between Sorel and St. Mathias, the St. Charles battle ground can still be traced. The battle took place on 25 November, but the actions of the Lower Canadian rebellion began on 7 May. On that day, some *Patriotes* met at St. Ours, on the lower Richelieu, and elected Papineau their leader, although he had been giving leadership for some time. Rebellion came a step closer when on 23 October, at St. Charles, *Patriotes* of the Richelieu Valley met and adopted thirteen resolutions similar to the Declaration of the Rights of Man. The chairman was Dr. Wolfred Nelson of St. Denis, a man who would play an active part in the rising. Despite his English name, culturally he was more French than English.

Papineau organized the youngest members of his *Patriote* party into a civil and a military wing. The commander of the military wing was Thomas Storrow Brown, a hardware merchant of Montreal who had gone bankrupt. The civil wing could also be converted quickly for military action. It was organized in six sections, each with a head. The sections corresponded with the six military districts of the Montreal area. Each section could become a battalion when required.

The *Patriotes* established two headquaters on the Richelieu, one at St. Denis where Dr. Nelson lived, and one at St. Charles, twelve kilometres to the south. There, Thomas Brown had his headquarters in the brick manor house of Pierre Dominique Debartzch, the Seigneur of St. Charles who had fought at the Battle of Chateauguay in 1813. Until 1832, Debartzch, who was of Polish extraction, had supported Papineau, but later after he was appointed to the Legislative Council, the seigneur turned against the radicals and began informing the governor general, Lord Gosfield, about *Patriote* doings. The *Patriotes* were strong enough in the Richelieu Valley to take Debartzch and his family prisoner. They then allowed the family to go to Quebec City, and they confiscated the seigneury, which could provide plenty of food for a military force. The house was turned into a barracks, and the drawing room became the guard room. Prisoners were brought to St. Charles because the house and some other buildings were safe places of incarceration where they were not likely to be rescued.

St. Charles (Lower Canada) 1837

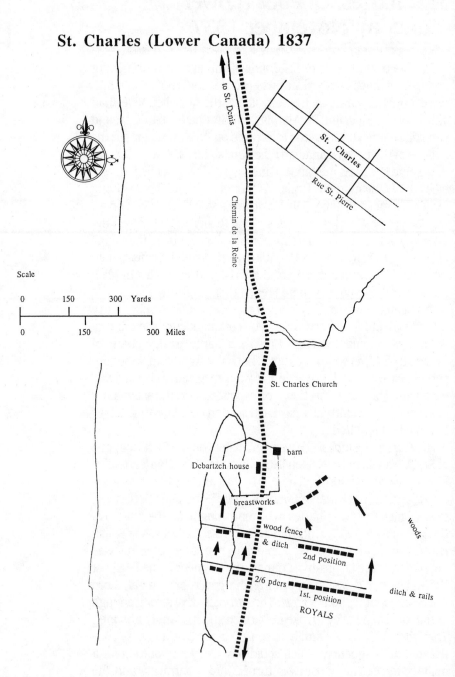

The Battle of St. Charles was fought stage by stage from south of the Debartzch house. Wetherall's troops moved north, taking positions at a ditch, than along a wood fence before moving on the rebel breastworks.

The fort and church at Chambly, Lower Canada, in 1838. Water colour by Philip J. Bainbrigge.

The *Patriotes* surrounded the Debartzch house with breastworks and turned a large area around it into a fortified camp.

The commander of forces was Lieutenant-General Sir John Colborne, who was posted to Lower Canada because the governor general was a civilian. Colborne's regular force was small to cope with a Lower Canadian population of some 650,000. At Quebec City were the 15th, part ot the 66th, the 79th and 83rd Regiments of Foot, and the 1st Royal Regiment, which Colborne dispatched to Montreal. Before he moved the 1st Royal there the garrison at Montreal district was the 32nd Regiment, while detachments of the 66th were at Ile aux Noix and Sorel. At St. Helen's Island, in the St. Lawrence River, were some Royal Artillerymen. When a clash between the *Fils de la Liberté* led by Thomas Storrow Brown and members of the English Canadian Doric Club occurred in the streets of Montreal on 6 November, Colborne ordered the 24th Regiment, stationed at Toronto and Kingston, to Montreal.

Hoping to end rebellion before it started, Colborne dispatched forces from two directions into the Richelieu Valley. One, under his quartermaster-general, Sir Charles Gore, went by streamer from Montreal to Sorel on the night of 22 November. With Gore went the flank companies of the 24th, a detachment of Royal Artillerymen and one 12-pounder howitzer, and some Royal Montreal Cavalry. Colborne sent magistrates with warrants for the arrest of key *Patriotes*. At that stage, Colborne wanted to avoid armed clashes, hoping that the show of might would deter the rebels. The second force, which was to join Gore's near St. Denis, under Lieutenant-Colonel George Wetherall of the 1st Royal Regiment, consisted of three companies of the Royals, one company of the 66th, twenty Royal Montreal Calvary under Captain Eléazar David, and a detachment of Royal Artillery with two 6-pounder guns under Captain John Glasgow, in all some 350 men. Wetherall's men were accompanied by two magistrates.

Rain teemed down as the force crossed the Chambly basin and marched north on a road becoming ever more muddy. The men marched only five kilometres in three hours. Upon reaching the

A fortified pass. Wetherall's troops were advancing to the capture of St. Charles, 25 November 1837. From a sketch by Beauclerk lithographed by N. Hartnell.

village of St. Hilaire, fifteen kilometres south of St. Charles, Wetherall was happy to halt his men and accept the hospitality of the Honourable Daniel de Hertel, the Seigneur de Rouville. Wetherall's decision not to proceed, while understandable, had fatal consequences for Gore's force at St. Denis. Unsupported by Wetherall's attack on St. Charles, Gore was defeated by the *Patriotes*, who captured the howitzer.

On 23 November, Wetherall received word of Gore's defeat, but he was unable to communicate with Colborne for four days. *Patriotes* were thick on the ground, but messengers Wetherall sent to Chambly asking for reinforcements got through. The grenadier company of the 1st Royals left in a scow for St. Hilaire. The following day, Brown took a strong party five kilometres south of St. Charles, destroyed a bridge over a stream that entered the Richelieu, and set up an advance guard and pickets. This force was commanded by Bonaventure Viger, a *Patriote* captain, who deployed his pickets on both sides of the stream and in buildings and woods. Viger was under orders to fire on Wetherall's regulars as soon as he spotted them, and to come to warn Brown. The latter had rail fences built some 250 metres south of the Debartzch house, in the centre of his fortified camp. Brown unwisely admitted a government spy into the camp and pressed him into service. The man escaped and went straight to Montreal to report on the *Patriote* situation.

Saturday 25 November was clear and cold. That day Colborne sent an order to Wetherall to withdraw to Montreal rather than risk being defeated. The message was intercepted and never reached Wetherall. Now that he was reinforced by the arrival of his grenadier company, and his other men were well rested and fed, he set out for St. Charles, his progress slowed by the need to repair bridges. An annoyance was the pickets who fired from both sides of the Richelieu, and one of the Royals was wounded. As the regulars marched, pickets left their posts and took up new ones in houses along the way. To drive away the marksmen, Wetherall's men set fire to buildings, so that their passage was betrayed by columns of smoke rising in the still air. Wetherall sent a farmer to ask the rebels for a parlay, but the man did not return.

In the armed camp at the Debartzch house, one of Brown's section heads, Dr. Henri-Alphonse Gauvin of Montreal, saw smoke

Beauclerk sketch of Wetherall's troops bivouacking at the Manor of St. Hilaire, 23 and 24 November 1837.

and heard a cannon boom. A ball flew by and struck the steeple of St. Charles church, north of the camp. Brown, taken by surprise, since he was in the village of St. Charles arranging for food to be sent to the camp, hurried back to the Debartzch house. He had seen Colborne's order, and he assumed that Wetherall was on his way back to Montreal. Brown did not realize that an order not received could not be obeyed. Wetherall's force now numbered 406 regulars, and 20 cavalrymen, Brown's amounted to 200 to 250 stationed in and around the Debartzch house or on picket duty.

To avoid the pickets, and a gun Brown had placed on the main road, the regulars marched inland to the east, through ploughed fields. Many civilians fled at the sight of Wetherall's force. Brown ordered some of his men to take up a position behind a solid wooden fence with a ditch, about 100 metres south of the camp, and to fire on Wetherall's advance force.

When Wetherall arrived at the fence Brown's men had built, he divided his force in two, separated by the two 6-pounder guns which he placed just east of the road. A small detachment was west of the road, the rest to the east of the guns. Gauvin, who commanded the men behind the sturdier wooden fence, raced back to the fortified manor to warn Brown. The *Patriotes* fired muskets, and Wetherall's artillery commander, Captain John Glasgow, replied with shells, grape and cannister shot. Brown ordered Rodolphe Desrivières, one of his section heads, to take an armed party to the rear and try to stop more inhabitants fleeing. Their behavior might convince Wetherall that the entire community was in a panic.

A farmer reported to Brown that the 'English general' wanted to parlay, and he would not harm anyone if he was allowed to pass by. Brown assumed that *Patriotes* from Pointe Olivier, across from Chambly, were pressing on Wetherall's rearguard, and he sent a message to Wetherall that his men could pass by if they laid down their arms. Since Brown had not agreed to parlay, Wetherall ordered the regulars to march towards what became their second position, against the wooden fence some 100 metres from the fortified camp's breastworks. The *Patriotes'* fire was devastating and Wetherall had his men lie down for protection. The *Patriotes* who had defended the wooden fence, commanded by Lieutenant Eusèbe Durocher and a former magazine editor named Siméon Marchessault, withdrew to their breastworks.

Wetherall's men moved forward and took the *Patriotes* former position. From the regulars' right, Desrivières' men were firing on them from woods beyond the ploughed fields. The regulars tried to storm Desrivières' men but were forced back, and Wetherall's horse was shot from under him. After some two hours of indecisive action, Wetherall ordered his three central companies to fix bayonets and charge the breastwork. The *Patriotes* had abatis in front of the log breastworks, but since the wall was less than one and one half metres high, the Royals had little difficulty climbing over and entering the camp.

The *Patriotes* were driven from their breastwork positions and the desperate struggle was now in the camp. Acccording to one story, fifty *Patriotes* pretended to surrender but attacked, precipitating a massacre by Wetherall's troops. Another source maintains that the *Patriotes* asked for quarter but they were slaughtered. Siméon Marchessault galloped to the village to free his animals and gather up his papers before fleeing. Bonaventure Viger swam across the icy Richelieu to escape. When the fight was over, Wetherall counted fifty-six bodies, but he thought that more corpses were in the burnt buildings. The regulars admitted that the *Patriotes* had fought with determination and courage. British losses were three regulars killed, ten wounded seriously and eight wounded slightly.

Wetherall had all the buildings within the fortified camp burnt except the Debartzch house, which had been damaged on the

Lieutenant-Colonel George Wetherall, commander of the British and Canadian troops at St. Charles, 25 November 1837.

outside by cannon fire, and on the inside by the *Patriote* occupation. Wetherall took twenty-five prisoners who were held in the St. Charles church. The wounded of both sides were cared for in the presbytery of the church by Lieutenant Edward Wetherall, the commanding officer's nephew.

At the time of the capitulation, Brown was 1,000 metres in the rear, near St. Charles village, trying to persuade anyone he found to come to the aid of the camp. When he thought that all was lost, he galloped to St. Denis, where Nelson blamed him for not holding Wetherall in check and relieved him of command. After the battle Wetherall waited until the 27th for orders from Colborne. Then, fearing an attack by *Patriotes* from Pointe Olivier, he ordered a withdrawal towards Chambly. When his force was off Pointe Olivier, the regulars traded shots with some *Patriotes* there.

The battle of St. Charles did not deter the *Patriotes*. But their ardour was cooled on 14 December when two brigades of regulars under Sir John Colborne attacked them at St. Eustache, northwest of Montreal. One brigade was led by Sir John Maitland, the lieutenant-colonel of the 32nd Regiment. The other was commanded by Lieutenant-Colonel Wetherall. The *Patriote* leaders were Amury Girod and Dr. Jean-Olivier Chénier. The doctor and 70 of his followers were killed, and 118 *Patriotes* were taken prisoner. A year passed before the *Patriotes* rose again in rebellion. The second rising was also crushed. Of the prisoners captured, twelve were hanged and fifty-eight were transported to penal colonies in Australia.

Today the church where the *Patriote* prisoners were confined remains and so does the manor house at St. Hilaire that belonged to the Seigneur de Rouville. Visitors may take walking tours of St. Denis to see the landmarks from the rebellion era. But the Debartzch house is no more. It was so badly damaged that the family never returned and it was later demolished.

Windmill Point, Prescott,
November 1838

14

The Upper Canadian rebellions could be called a tempest in a teacup. Much more alarming were the raids staged by Canadian rebels and American sympathizers. The latter believed that their northern neighbours longed for their own independence movement. By the autumn of 1838, Americans were forming what they called Hunters Lodges, imitating the Lower Canadians' societies of *frères chasseurs*, and styling themselves patriots. Because of the threat the raids posed, by December 1838 the British government had poured nine regiments of regular troops, a detachment of Royal Marines, and 200 sailors from the Royal Navy into Upper Canada. The so-called patriots staged many raids, and the Battle of the Windmill was one of the most serious and prolonged, although it had its comic moments.

Two historic sites relate to the Battle of the Windmill. One is Fort Wellington, on the east side of Prescott, and the other is the windmill itself. It stands close to the shore of the St. Lawrence River just east of Wexford, a tiny hamlet below Prescott. A side road leads to the site. The windmill now resembles an old lighthouse, because it was converted to one forty-one years after the battle. The actual battle ground is rather overgrown, and the buildings of the hamlet of New Jerusalem have for the most part vanished. The activity on the river is easy to envisage, and a good vantage point is the Ogdensburg waterfront.

On Sunday 11 November 1838, about 400 patriots left Sackets Harbor and other New York ports of call bound for Prescott. Their objective was the capture of Fort Wellington, to cut off communication with Lower Canada. Thus they thought they could starve the few Tory opponents of freedom and their British soldier allies in the upper province into submission. Their leader was 'General' John Ward Birge of the Onondaga County Hunters Lodge, formed around Salina and Syracuse, New York. Birge appears not to have known about the Rideau Canal, the alternate route to the St. Lawrence, then well patrolled by British regulars and Canadian militia.

While Birge was appealing to Hunters in Onondaga County, 'Colonel' Martin Woodruff of Watertown and 'Colonel' Dorrephus Abbey of Pamelia were busy recruiting in Jefferson County. The man who would ultimately lead the attack was Nils von Schoultz, who had deliberately thrown a smokescreen over his past life.

Battle of the Windmill

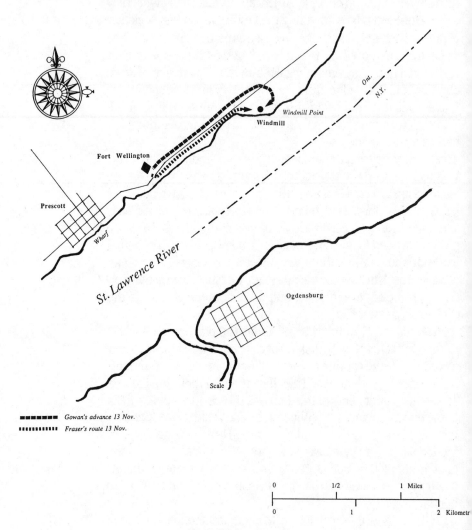

The first attempt to capture the windmill, on 13 November, failed. More reinforcements, both militia volunteers and British regulars, soon discouraged the invaders from holding out after the 16th.

The American steamer United States *that was impounded by the United States marshall for transporting patriot invaders to Ogdensburg, N.Y.*

Von Schoultz at the time was a romantic hero to Americans, and he also found much sympathy among Canadians. The story he told was web of fact and fiction. He claimed to be an exile from Poland, a onetime officer in the Polish army who had fought the Russians in 1830. He saw the oppressed Canadians as suffering the fate of the peasants of Poland, and he resolved to help them throw off the British yoke of slavery. He was a devout Roman Catholic with a *fiancée* in Syracuse. Not until the 1960s was von Schoultz unmasked. His great grandaughter, Ella Pipping, broke silence after 130 years when she read the contents of a packet that had remained unopened by his embarrassed family in Sweden.

Pipping entitled her biography *Solider of Fortune*. She revealed that Von Schoultz was Finnish-born and a Swedish national who, for a time had held a commission in the Polish army. He had a wife and two small daughters in Stockholm. He had dabbled in chemistry as a hobby, but he was not well educated. Unable to support his family adequately, he went to London, England, to seek employment. On impulse and to shirk his responsibilities, he boarded a ship for New York, and pretending to be qualified chemist, obtained a job in a salt manufacturing plant in Salina.

Von Schoultz left with other members of his lodge for Sackets Harbor, the main rallying point for the invading Hunters. Beforehand, some patriots had seized two Lake Ontario schooners, both named *Charlotte*, one registered at Toronto, the other at Oswego. On the morning of 11 November, the American steamer *United States*, with Captain James Van Cleeve in command, was downbound for Ogdensburg when it stopped at Sackets Harbor. Nearly 400 men went on board, while others joined the steamer at Cape Vincent, Clayton and Millen's Bay, all regular stops. Off Millen's Bay, Van Cleeve agreed to take the two schooners in tow, the patriots on the *United States* remaining hidden below. Van Cleeve was not surprised at being asked to tow the schooners, for the breeze was light. He had often aided sailing craft in the past. After the schooners had been made fast to the sides of the steamer, the Hunters emerged, clad in a bewildering array of home-made uniforms, no two alike.

One who had come aboard at Clayton was Bill Johnston, Canadian-born but very anti-British, and known as the Pirate of the Thousand Islands. Bill was the admiral of the patriots' navy in the east. Six months before, in May, he had captured the Canadian steamer *Sir Robert Peel* for his flagship. When he could not start the engine, he burned the steamer.

As the *United States* approached Morristown the breeze freshened from the southwest. Some patriots transferred to the schooners. Bill Johnston, as the admiral, took command of the *Charlotte of Oswego*. By then the patriots who had remained on the *United States* were having second thoughts, and decided not to take part in the attack. Before resuming his downward way, Van Cleeve sent a message to the magistrate at Ogdensburg and another to Brockville, where the occupants of a blockhouse on an island close by were watching the proceedings with more than passing interest. The schooners, sailing in a fair wind, reached Ogdensburg, where Birge had himself rowed ashore in a gig, claiming he would return with recruits.

As the two schooners began to cross towards Prescott, Bill Johnston showed that he was no more competent in a sailing vessel

Bill Johnston, the 'Commodore of the Patriot Navy in the East'. This representation of Johnston was made by Lossing in his field book on the War of 1812.

than in the steamer *Sir Robert Peel*. He ran the *Charlotte of Oswego* aground on the muddy delta of the Oswegatchie River. The *Charlotte of Toronto* tacked back and forth waiting for it to refloat. General Birge had himself rowed out to the *Charlotte of Toronto*, and the officers argued over what should be done. Nils von Schoultz wanted to capture Fort Wellington at once, but Birge vetoed the suggestion. Pleading illness, Birge returned to Ogdensburg.

Von Shoultz took command of the men on the *Charlotte of Toronto*, and sailing above Prescott he landed a party at Honeywell's Bay. The Hunters captured two militia dragoons and after blocking the road for a while, and destroying a bridge, they returned to the schooner.

The patriots now decided to attack Prescott, and they succeeded in tying up at the wharf, but the rope broke and the schooner drifted downstream. Sentries alerted some militia billeted in the village, and they began dragging a cannon towards the wharf. They managed to load and fire before the ship was out of range. The time was now 2.00 a.m. on 12 November. The shot was heard in Fort Wellington, where Lieutenant-Colonel Plomer Young, a British regular officer, was in command. The garrison in the village was 200 embodied Grenville militiamen, that in the fort thirty-five Glengarry militia. Most were soon dressed and ready for action.

The shot was also heard in Brockville, which, coupled with the warning sent by Captain Van Cleeve of the *United States*, alerted the Grand Master of the Loyal Orange Lodge, Ogle Robert Gowan. He was also the commander of a newly authorized 9th provisional battalion of militia which he had named the Queen's Loyal Borderers. Already embodied were 200 of the 1st Leeds Regiment and the cavalry squadron of thirty dragoons. A detachment set out for Prescott, seventeen kilometres off. At dawn the Reverend Robert Blakely, rector of Prescott, learned that some of von Schoultz's men had landed, and thinking that they were still blocking the road he set out on horseback by an inland route, arriving in Brockville at 10.00 a.m. to warn his friend Gowan of the intruders. The Orange leader was preparing to leave with two companies of his battalion, and he promised to open the road.

Meanwhile, a scow came out from Ogdensburg, and guns carried by the grounded *Charlotte of Oswego* were placed in it. The *Charlotte of Toronto* took the scow in tow, and aboard the schooner the patriot leaders again argued over the next move. The quarrel was settled when the schooner ran aground off Windmill Point. If the force was to land at all now, it had to be near the stone tower. But the site looked promising. Surrounding the windmill was the tiny hamlet of New Jerusalem, whose stone houses and walls could be used as cover. The walls of the six-storey tall mill were thick and at openings near the top, von Schoultz could station snipers. Three small field guns, small arms and ammunition were loaded into lifeboats and 192 men – twenty-two of them British subjects – went ashore.

Ogle Robert Gowan, the lieutenant-colonel of the Queen's Royal Borderers, the name he gave his 9th Provisional Battalion. Gowan commanded the right wing at the battle on 13 November 1838.

Freed of her heavy cargo and passengers, the *Charlotte of Toronto* floated, and her crew beat a hasty retreat up the river. The patriots had coerced the crew into taking them aboard in the first place. Soon afterwards the steamer *Experiment*, commanded by Lieutenant William Fowell, Royal Navy, arrived from Brockville and began patrolling between Windmill Point and Ogdensburg, which ensured that no other Hunters would reach the windmill for the moment. The *United States* and the much smaller steamer *Paul Pry*, had been trying to pull the *Charlotte of Oswego* off the bottom. The *Experiment* with her 18-pounder gun and a 3-pounder swivel gun, soon chased the two unarmed steamers into Ogdensburg harbour. The magistrate there sent a message to Fowell, asking him not to fire in American waters.

At the windmill the patriots voted to make von Schoultz their leader. To avoid bickering, von Schoultz agreed to have two seconds-in-command – Martin Woodruff and Dorrephus Abbey. The patriots occupied the windmill, and when the inhabitants of New Jerusalem fled, they took over the stone buildings as well. They hoisted the blue banner of the Onondaga lodge, emblazened with the words 'Liberated by the Onondaga Hunters' and waited for thousands of Canadian supporters to join them. But quite the reverse was taking place.

Ogle Gowan had left Brockville at 1.00 p.m., and his men stopped to repair the bridge which the patriots had demolished at Honeywell's Bay, before they continued on to Prescott. They joined the Grenville militiamen posted near the windmill, and more reinforcements were on the way. Lieutenant-Colonel Philip Vankoughnett arrived with some Stormont men, and 300 from

The British armed steamer Experiment, *commanded by Lieutenant William Fowell, R.N. at the Battle of the Windmill, drawn by C.H.J. Snider.*

Dundas and 150 from Glengarry joined what was becoming a thickening circle surrounding the windmill and the buildings of New Jerusalem. By nightfall on Monday the 12th, the armed steamers *Queen Victoria* and *Cobourg* arrived from Kingston, with Captain William Sandom of the Royal Navy in command, bringing seventy-four regulars from the 83rd Regiment under Lieutenant William Johnson, and thirty Royal Marines led by Lieutenant Charles Parker.

Nils von Schoultz, leader of the so-called patriots at the Windmill. He professed to be a Polish exile, but he was a Swedish national and something of a cad.

By this time the governor of New York State, William Marcy, was taking steps to limit the size of the border infraction. He sent a courier to Sackets Harbor ordering Nathaniel Garrow, a United States marshal, and Colonel William Worth of the United States Army to take two companies of American regulars to Ogdensburg. No more patriots were to be allowed to cross the river. The two officers arrived on the night of the 12th, and Garrow seized the *Charlotte of Oswego* and the steamers *United States* and *Paul Pry* for violations of the Neutrality Act.

A drizzling rain was falling, and the militiamen and regulars posted around the windmill spent a miserable night. On the morning of the 13th, Lieutenant-Colonel Young resolved on action, partly because the men could not remain in such uncomfortable circumstances much longer. He ordered an attack in two columns, the right one under Lieutenant-Colonel Gowan, the left under Lieutenant-Colonel Richard Duncan Fraser of the 2nd Grenville Regiment. Gowan's vanguard, of forty-four from the 83rd Regiment, was commanded by Lieutenant William Johnson. Fraser's was thirty Royal Marines under Lieutenant Charles Parker. Gowan's column advanced from Fort Wellington along the shore. Fraser's swung inland to approach the windmill from the east. By the time the men marched, Lieutenant Fowell, aboard the *Experiment*, was directing firing from all three steamers against the windmill.

Von Schoultz watched the columns moving into line of battle with dismay. What he hoped were reinforcements coming to his flag was an attacking force. He ordered his men out in open order and to hold their fire until he gave the word. Excited at the prospect of action, the patriots ignored their leader and began firing almost at once. The regulars drew together, flanked one another and forced the patriots to take cover behind the buildings, and then to dash for the windmill. By this time, ironically, cannon balls from Captain Sandom's two steamers were doing more damage to the militia and regulars than to the invaders. The windmill stood on a bluff, and the gunners had to aim high.

After the first assault, Lieutenant-Colonel Young called off further attempts, to avoid more casualties. The cannon balls which struck the windmill were bouncing off the thick walls. The *Experiment's* 18-pounder might have inflicted damage, but the steamer had

View of the Battle of the Windmill, below Prescott, from Ogdensburg, N.Y. The sketch was made after the arrival of the steamers Victoria *and* Cobourg *from Kingston.*

developed engine trouble and had limped into Prescott for repairs. The regulars and militia withdrew out of range of von Schoultz's marksmen at upper windows in the windmill. Young sent a request to Kingston for heavier guns.

Under a flag of truce, both sides picked up their dead and wounded. Lieutenant William Johnson of the 83rd Regiment, and Lieutenant John Dulmage of the 1st Grenville Regiment, had been killed. Six rank and file of the regulars were dead, and eighteen wounded. Militia losses were thirteen dead and fifty-one wounded. Hunter losses were perhaps thirteen dead and twenty-eight wounded, and because theirs was to be a bloodless coup, they had not brought any medical supplies.

The people of Ogdensburg were very excited, watching from a ringside seat. Earlier, some patriots had managed to join von Schoultz, but now Marshal Garrow and Colonel Worth were stopping their attempts to communicate with the men in the windmill. Von Schoultz's situation was worsening, for some of his men had deserted and had succeeded in reaching the American shore. That night a man named Meredith paddled across the icy water on a plank, conferred with von Schoultz, and returned to Ogdensburg to report the situation. Meredith told General Birge of the plight of he wounded, lying untended in the windmill. Birge suggested that Bill Johnston create a diversion by attacking Gananoque, but the pirate had vanished. Rewards had been posted for his capture after he burned the *Peel*, and he left when the marshal arrived .

On Thursday 15 November, Colonel Worth and Lieutenant-Colonel Young met aboard the American steamer *Telegraph* under a flag of truce. Worth asked Young to allow the patriots at the windmill to go to the American side in return for his pledge that the United States Army would prevent further invasions. Young refused, because he did not have permission from the lieutenant-governor of Upper Canada, Sir George Arthur.

That night the steamer *Paul Pry* slipped out of Ogdensburg harbour carrying the postmaster, Preston King, and others. King tried to persuade von Schoultz to evacuate the windmill, but one of the men who had come on the steamer quietly informed him that reinforcements would be coming. Martin Woodruff and Dorrephus Abbey refused to leave, and *Paul Pry* returned to Ogdensburg taking some of the wounded, and the last chance to escape was lost.

On 16 November, Lieutenant-Colonel Henry Dundas arrived from Kingston with four fresh companies of his 83rd Regiment, Major Forbes Macbean of the Royal Artillery, two 18-pounder guns and a howitzer. From Beauharnois, the commander of forces in both the Canadas, Sir John Colborne, sent the grenadier company of 93rd Regiment. The 93rd was a Highland unit, and the men wore the feathered bonnet, and the kilt and plaid of Black Watch tartan.

One of the 18-pounders was placed behind the windmill, the howitzer and the other 18-pounder on gunboats. These opened fire doing little damage, but von Schoultz had had enough and he ordered a white flag flown from the top of the mill. Even after it was in place the shooting continued. The blue flag of the Onondaga Hunters was still flying, and the first man who tried to haul it down was shot. Then Dundas ordered a temporary ceasefire in order to call on the invaders to surrender.

At the call, Martin Woodruff ran out of the windmill frantically waving a white cloth, begging the troops to hold their fire. As the Hunters filed out, infuriated militiamen began to abuse them, and Dundas ordered his regulars to protect them. Many patriots and British officers were asking about von Schoultz, but he was not to be found. He had slipped away and vanished. Later, Eustice Fell and Edward Smith of the Prescott independent company found the wretched Swede skulking in some bushes near the river, and marched him off to Prescott where the other prisoners had been taken. Some 160 Hunters or Canadian rebels were put aboard the steamer *Cobourg* for transport to Kingston, after a march through lines of hostile Prescott citizens.

At Kingston the prisoners were roped together in a long line with von Schoultz in the lead. Again they moved between lines of angry

Uniforms of the 93rd (Highland) Foot. One company was sent from Montreal to the Battle of the Windmill. The rest of the regiment was in Toronto by the end of December 1838.

Sketch of Prescott by George Harlow White, drawn in August 1876. By that time the windmill had been converted into a lighthouse.

faces, protected by regulars, the band of the 83rd Regiment playing an ironic 'Yankee Doodle'. At Fort Henry they were confined in large barrack rooms, and fifty who were under twenty-one were segregated from the rest. Sir George Arthur decided that the under-aged prisoners could be paroled to their homes. The older prisoners would be tried by a military court martial commencing on 28 November in Kingston.

Before the court martials took place, the dead were buried. Of the many funerals, Lieutenant William Johnson's attracted the most attention. The cortège started from the Tête du Pont barracks, the band of his own 83rd Regiment playing. Many of Kingston's leading citizens followed, and after them the men of the 83rd with black crepe on their shakos. Men of the Royal Navy and some militia units followed. Afterwards a cannon and a detachment of militia were stationed at the windmill where Johnson fell, to discourage patriot landings.

Following the military court martial in Kingston, eleven Hunters were executed. Von Schoultz was hanged at Fort Henry, Martin Woodruff, Dorrephus Abbey and eight others at the Kingston jail. Afterwards, someone who knew of von Schoultz's true origins gathered up his papers and the newspaper reports and sent them to his widow in Sweden, where they lay unopened for more than a century.

The Fenians

The Battle of Ridgeway. The Fenians are on the left with their Irish harp flag. Both sides, especially the Fenians, are too well dressed, with their Union army uniforms in such good shape.

The Fenian Brotherhood, the American branch of the Irish Republican Brotherhood, was founded in New York City in 1859 to foster Irish independence from Great Britain. The name 'Fenian' derived from the Gaelic 'Fianna' — warriors of the ancient King Finn. The movement was small until the closing months of the United States Civil War, a time when northern resentment against Britain for favouring the South was running high. Many Irishmen had enlisted in the Union Army, and when they were demobilized the brotherhood was in a position to found a Fenian army of experienced veterans. By that time, too, the American Fenians had wearied of the original plan to finance and equip rebels in Ireland, and were looking for a more direct way of striking at Britain.

John A. Macdonald, then the attorney general of Canada West, kept himself well informed on Fenian doings and was very much aware that they had designs on Canadian territory. Fenians were talkative, especially in the bars where they held their meetings, and spies had no difficulty infiltrating the movement. In March 1866, as groups of Fenians made their way to border towns and cities, Ottawa called for 10,000 militiamen to support the small garrisons of British regular troops stationed in Canada and 14,000 men responded.

The Fenians launched five raids, all told, and in three of these attempts they succeeded in crossing into Canada. The first, foiled by a United States revenue vessel, was an attempted landing on Campobello Island, New Brunswick. When the steamboat (which had been purchased by the brotherhood) was intercepted, the Fenians turned back. The second raid, of 1-3 June 1866, and the most serious, ended in the Battle of Ridgeway. The third was a crossing from Vermont into southern Quebec, where the Fenians were more easily dispersed. The fourth occurred in 1870, again into southern Quebec. The fifth was against Manitoba in 1871, and it was stopped by United States troops.

Canadian volunteers at Thorold, Niagara peninsula, in 1866. When the government called for 10,000 men to fight the Fenians, 14,000 responded.

Ridgeway 1866

Ridgeway lies on Highway 3 between Port Colborne and Fort Erie, Ontario. The site of the battle is found above the intersection of the highway and Ridge Road, which runs north out of Ridgeway. Two concession lines north of Highway 3C is Garrison Road. A marker stands on the north side of Garrison Road less than a kilometre east of Ridge Road. This marker is at the southern end of the battle ground. The intersection of Ridge Road with Bertie Road, the concession line north of Garrison Road, was the centre of the battle. The Fenians' main position was almost a concession breadth north of Bertie Road, and the southernmost pickets were to the south of Bertie Road. The Fenian main position was around the base of the ridge standing some thirty metres above the surrounding landscape. The site was well-chosen, with a clear view down Ridge Road, a spot selected by an experienced military commander, a veteran of the American Civil War and now a lieutenant-colonel in the Fenian army, John O'Neill.

O'Neill's invasion was to have been part of a much larger series of raids, but his was the only one to materialize in Canada West. His force of from 800 to 1,000 men was made up of the 13th Regiment — O'Neill's own — from Tennessee, the 17th from Kentucky (Colonel Owen Starr), the 7th from Buffalo (Colonel John Hoye) and the 18th from Ohio (Colonel John Grace), as well as some men from Indiana.

In the early hours of 1 June, they crossed the Niagara River in four scows towed by tugs, hired as transports, landed at Freeburgh's wharf near the mouth of Frenchman's Creek, and set up camp on Newbigging's farm nearby. While some of them erected breastworks, others went horse stealing — mounts to use for scouting. Still others went into Fort Erie and coerced the reeve and the council into providing them with food. After 10 a.m., on hearing that soldiers were coming by rail from Port Colborne, the Fenians broke camp and moved north to the mouth of Black Creek where they bivouacked for the night.

The Canadian government was already responding to the situation. Even before anyone knew of O'Neill's plans, a call to arms had been telegraphed from Ottawa to the commanders of all the military districts. Militia units destined for the Niagara Peninsula were Toronto's 2nd Battalion Queen's Own Rifles (acting Lieutenant-Colonel John S. Dennis), 480 strong, the 10th Royals

Troop Movements Before the Battle of Ridgeway

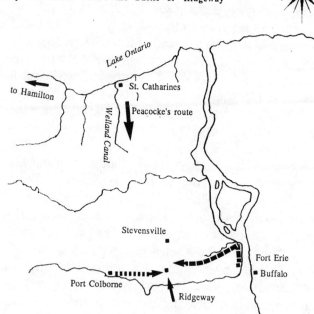

Lake Ontario

to Hamilton

St. Catharines

Welland Canal

Peacocke's route

Stevensville

Fort Erie

Buffalo

Port Colborne

Ridgeway

Lake Erie

IIIIIIIIIII Booker's route

▮▬▬▬▬▬ O'Neill's march

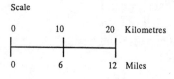

Scale

| 0 | 10 | 20 | Kilometres |

| 0 | 6 | 12 | Miles |

*The setting for the Battle of Ridgeway was the eastern portion of the Niagara peninsula, involving St.
Catharines, Fort Erie and Port Colborne.*

212

and the York Rifle Company. The 13th (infantry) Battalion of Hamilton (Lieutenant Colonel Alfred Booker), the 19th Battalion (Lieutenant-Colonel James Currie of St. Catharines), and the Caledonia Rifle Company were among the local units posted for duty. The commander of forces in Canada West was a British regular officer, Major-General George Napier, whose headquarters were in Toronto. The Adjutant-General of Militia was Colonel P.L. Macdougall. Two regular regiments were on duty in the province — the 47th, stationed at Toronto, and the 16th, at London.

By 1 June, General Napier had two field forces positioned to deal with O'Neill and his Fenians. The commander of the regulars was Colonel George Peacocke of the 16th Regiment, who left London by rail for Hamilton with 200 of his men.

Three companies of the 47th Regiment left Toronto for Port Dalhousie by steamer, along with the Grey Battery of Royal Artillery. The regulars were to gather at St. Catharines, where Lieutenant-Colonel Currie was marshalling his 19th Battalion to join them.

The second field force was solely of militia, and commanded by Lieutenant-Colonel Alfred Booker of the 13th Battalion from Hamilton. In addition to his own battalion, Booker's force included the 2nd batallion Queen's Own Rifles under Lieutenant-Colonel John S. Dennis (who was given the command because the battalion's own commander, William S. Durie, was serving as a staff officer), the York Rifle Company (Captain Robert Davis) and the Caledonia Rifle Company (Captain William Jackson). Booker took his force by rail to Port Colborne. From there, and from St. Catharines, Lieutenant Colonel Peacocke, the regular officer and Booker's superior, could surround the Fenians near Fort Erie.

Around midnight, Peacocke sent Captain C.S. Akers of the Royal Engineers to Booker, with orders to proceed to Ridgeway and march north to meet the main force from St. Catharines at Stevensville. By the time Akers arrived, Booker and Dennis, his second-in-command, had information from the customs agents at Fort Erie that the Fenians were at the Newbiggings' farm (at Frenchman's Creek). Dennis convinced Booker that they should go directly to Fort Erie by rail. Booker then telegraphed Peacocke requesting permission for a change of plan. Peacocke had also instructed Booker to put men aboard a steamer and patrol the Niagara River. The *W.T. Robb* was chosen for this purpose, and the

Welland Field Battery and Dunnville Naval Brigade went aboard. Dennis sailed on the *W.T. Robb* under the impression that Peacocke would accept the proposed change of plan. Peacocke refused, and ordered Booker to follow his original orders to proceed to Ridgeway. Booker's force boarded the train and arrived at Ridgeway at 6.00 a.m. on 2 June.

Three factors contributed to the outcome of the Battle of Ridgeway. First, Colonel John O'Neill's sources of information were surprisingly accurate. Second, by early morning of 2 June, Colonel Peacocke's force was enlarged by two more companies of the 47th Regiment from Toronto and the St. Catharines field battery of artillery, and the 10th Royals from Toronto. Finding breakfast for everyone took time, and in consequence he was not able to keep to his schedule for the rendez-vous at Stevensville. Third, Booker started his march north from Ridgeway far too early. Soon after Booker set out, local farmers warned him that the Fenians were close and in front of him. He paid no attention for rumours of that nature abounded.

About the time that Booker's men were leaving Port Colborne, Lieutenant-Colonel O'Neill received word that Peacocke and Booker were about to join forces, and he resolved to deal with them one at a time. He roused his men at Black Creek, and they marched along a path that led southwest, coming in time to the ridge north of Bertie Road. Knowing a fine vantage point when he saw one,

Cartoon of Fenians at Ridgeway. Gauust Doscen wrote a contemporary history of the raids and illustrated it with cartoons suggesting that the invaders were better at drinking than fighting.

*Gauust Doscen drew this unflattering cartoon, again featuring drinking, to il-
lustrate his history of the Fenian raids.*

O'Neill chose the base of the ridge, with lookouts on top, for the
main body of his troops. Then he placed skirmishers and sharpshooters in forward positions, the foremost well south of Bertie
Road, on the east side of Ridge Road.

The Fenians were already lying in wait when they heard the
whistle of the train as it pulled into Ridgeway with Booker's force
aboard. Booker's men were poorly prepared but in high spirits.
Their uniforms were too heavy for a warm June morning, and food
was in short supply. Booker spent an hour finding wagons to carry
equipment. The only man with a horse was Booker himself. He
formed his column, choosing the Queen's Own Rifles as his
vanguard, now commanded by Major Charles Gillmor. The 5th
Company under Captain John Edwards was the spearhead, for that
company was equipped with Spencer repeating rifles. The York
Rifles followed, with Booker's 13th Battalion behind it under the
direct command of the major, James Skinner. The Caledonia Rifle
Company was the rearguard.

After a march of three kilometres, the vanguard signalled that the enemy had been spotted. Booker called a halt, and the column extended into battle line. The Queen's Own Rifles spread out from the 5th company's central location, the 1st company to its left and the 2nd company to its right as skirmishers. The 3rd, 4th,, 7th, and 8th companies gave support from behind or moved to the flanks, while the 9th (the Trinity College company) was sent to the far left of the line, and the 10th (of kilted Highlanders) to the far right. The York Rifles and the 13th Battalion also stayed back as reserves, while the Caledonia Rifle Company continued as the rearguard. The 10th company of the Queen's Own returned and was sent out a second time

The Queen's Own advanced rapidly and drove the Fenians from their advance pickets south of Bertie Road. The Toronto men bore the brunt of the Fenian sharpshooters until they were almost out

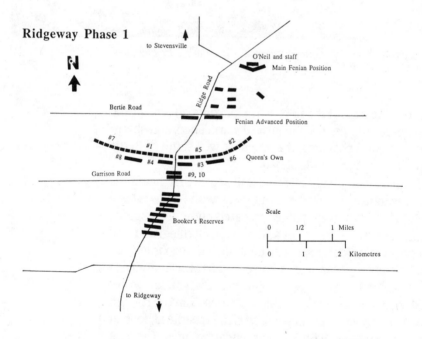

At the start of the battle the Queen's Own Rifles formed the Canadian advanced position, while the Fenian pickets extended to the south of Bertie Road.

of ammunition and Major Gillmor warned Booker that they needed to be relieved. Booker pulled the Queen's Own back and substituted the right wing of the 13th Battalion and the York Rifle Company, who advanced to Bertie Road, driving the Fenians back towards their main position.

The left wing of the 13th and the Caledonia Rifles continued in reserve, and Booker sent the 10th (Highland Company), of the Queen's Own into the woods to the right of the 13th to protect the flank. The kilted men rushed to obey, and set about clearing the woods of Fenians. Thus far, the Canadian militiamen were doing very well against O'Neill's veterans. The Fenians were thinking of giving up and retreating when a misunderstanding turned the tide. A few Fenians on their stolen horses rode into Gillmor's view. He reported to Booker, and on his order, Gillmor shouted, 'Prepare for Cavalry.'

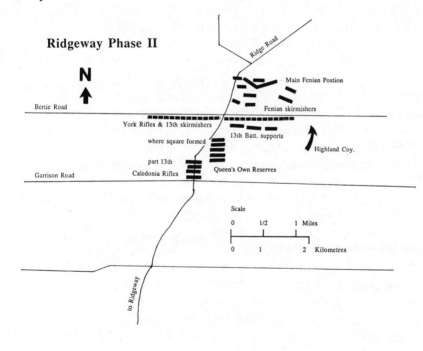

Just before the Canadians were thrown into confusion, the Queen's Own had been withdrawn to form the reserves, while the York Rifles and the 13th Infantry Battalion had taken up the advanced position.

The first eight companies of the Queen's Own, standing half way between Garrision and Bertie Roads, ran and formed three sides of a hollow square. When no more horsemen appeared, Booker saw his error and called the Queen's Own back into column, which created great confusion. Seeing the Queen's Own marching southwards, the left wing of the 13th Battalion, that had not yet been engaged, assumed that Booker had ordered a retreat and the men began to run back towards Ridgeway. Under the impression that his right flank was being turned, Booker gave in and ordered the buglers to sound the withdrawal. Amidst much disorder the poorly disciplined militia fled back to the railway station, and the return of the skirmishers added to the confusion.

Only minutes before, the militia had had O'Neill feeling uneasy and impressed by their steadiness. Now, much encouraged, the Fenians pursued the demoralised militiamen to the edge of Ridgeway, firing after them, checked only by groups of Canadians less demoralised than the majority, who rallied to fire back. With in sight of the railway station, O'Neill called off the pursuit. He knew the size of Peacocke's force, which might be near Stevensville by now, since it was nearly midday. O'Neill ordered his men to move towards Fort Erie, the opposite direction to Peacocke's line of advance. Booker had the wounded moved to the house of people named Baker, south of Garrison Road, until they could be taken to the train. By late in the afternoon, Booker and his force were back in Port Colborne, after an exhausting experience. In the battle, one ensign, three non-commissioned officers and five privates of the Queen's Own had been killed, and twenty-one-all ranks were wounded. Of the 13th Battalion, one private was killed and fifteen all ranks were wounded; one York Rifleman was also wounded. Except for Booker's error in thinking that the Fenians had cavalry, the Canadian militia might have won the Battle of Ridgeway.

A further skirmish occurred when the Fenians arrived at Fort Erie. Lieutenant-Colonel Dennis ordered the Welland and Dunnville men — 76 strong — from the *W.T. Robb* to resist the 800 Fenians. The volunteers were soon scattered; six were wounded, thirty-six captured, and eighteen ran down the river road and were taken abroad the *W.T. Robb*. The others, among them was Dennis, found hiding places in the village.

The Fenians spent the night encamped in the ruins of old Fort

Erie, but O'Neill had already made up his mind to return to the New York side of the river. Lieutenant-Colonel Peacocke and his regulars were certainly marching for Fort Erie, and O'Neill knew that his

Canada General Service Medal. Volunteers who served during the Fenian raids were awarded the medal, but not until the late 1890s when recruits were needed for the Boer War. One recipient was the author's grandfather, Private Thomas Edwin Seaman, 1st Company Brockville Rifles.

men would be no match for them.

In the early hours of Sunday 3 June, by a prearranged signal, a barge and two steam tugs crossed the Niagara River. A few stragglers and pickets remained on the Canadian side but these were soon found. The barge full of Fenians was arrested by law officers aboard the United States steam tug *Harrison* and escorted to Buffalo. There the prisoners on the barge were guarded by the United States revenue cutter *Michigan* to prevent escapes. The Fenians were not prosecuted, and were merely given railway tickets back to their homes. This leniency towards people who broke the United States neutrality laws encouraged further raids.

From a military standpoint, the Fenian raids were of no real significance; they were a nuisance that caused the government to waste large sums of money on preparations to combat them. In only one respect did the Fenian threat have a positive effect for Canada. The raids helped persuade New Brunswick of the benefits of Confederation with the other British North American colonies.

The Settlement of the Prairies

The execution of Ontario Orangeman Thomas Scott at Fort Garry, February 1870 by order of Louis Riel.

The two rebellions led by Louis Riel, the first in 1870 and the second in 1885, were caused by fears rising from the expansion of white settlement into the west. Settlements of semi-nomadic people — the offspring of fur traders and Indian women — evolved first at Red River (the site of Winnipeg) and later along the North and South branches of the Sasketchewan River. The people of French-Indian origin were the Métis, and those of Scots-Indian background were called mixed bloods. Both the Riel rebellions were the result of fear that rights would not be respected, and that the people would lose the lands they occupied — the long, narrow strip farms where they grew some crops to supplement their annual buffalo hunt.

The Red River colony had been founded by the Earl of Selkirk. But it was not a success for European settlers and it became the home of the Métis and mixed bloods whose families had worked in the fur trade. After 1836 the colony was governed by the Hudson's Bay Company, whose lands were to become part of the new Dominion of Canada in 1869, a transfer that was delayed by the first rebellion.

The negotiations for the change in sovereignty were carried out as though no one lived in the Hudson's Bay domain. The Métis became alarmed, and they turned for help to Louis Riel, who had received his education in Quebec. They looked to him because his father, Louis Sr., had been their leader before him. When surveyors from Canada ignored the lot lines of the Métis' farms, Riel took action. A band of Métis occupied Upper Fort Garry, and Riel formed a provisional government to negotiate the colony's entry into Canada.

Riel had the support of both the Métis and the mixed bloods, but some English-speaking Canadians who had moved into the colony opposed the provisional government. Riel's main blunder was to order the execution, by a firing squad, of an Orangeman from Ontario, Thomas Scott, for his part in attempting to capture Upper Fort Garry. The execution placed Prime Minister Sir John A. Macdonald between the voters of Ontario and of Quebec, and turned the event at Red River into a French-English, Catholic-Protestant confrontation.

Macdonald responded to the situation politically and militarily. His government passed the Manitoba Act in June 1870, which set up the province of Manitoba and granted the Métis many of their demands. However, to appease Ontario, Macdonald refused to grant amnesty to Riel. The prime minister also dispatched an expedition under Sir Garnet Wolseley to Red River. When Wolseley's force drew near in late August, Riel and other members of his government fled to the United States.

Although land was reserved for the Métis in Manitoba, most drifted away to form new settlements farther from civilization. They felt that they could continue their traditional way of life at a distance from the white settlers who were flocking into Manitoba. By the 1880s the Métis again felt that their way of life was being threatened as white settlers arrived. Nor were they reassured by the presence of detachments of the North West Mounted Police. The police were there to keep the peace between traders and the Indians who were the Métis relatives, and with whom they were on good terms. By 1884, two of the Mounties' posts were close to the Métis settlements — Fort Carlton near Duck Lake, and Fort Pitt near Frog Lake (inside the present Alberta boundary).

Louis Riel, the Métis leader, was a visionary rather than a military commander. By 1885 he could not be considered entirely sane.

Since his departure to the United States in 1870, Riel had been back periodically to Canada, and he spent time in mental institutions in Quebec. He had begun having had visions of a new Catholic state on the prairies. In 1884 he was teaching school in Montana when a delegation led by Gabriel Dumont came to ask him to accompany them to the Northwest to lead his people once more. With surveyors and settlers coming in ever greater numbers, the Métis could see the end of the buffalo hunt, reserves for the Indians, and their culture in jeopardy again. As in 1870, Sir John A. Macdonald failed to see that he needed to reconcile a small population of Métis and Indians to the march of settlement. The prime minister was preoccupied with plans for his transcontinental railway.

In the second rising, Riel did not draw as much support as in 1870. On the earlier occasion, the English-speaking mixed bloods had sided with his Métis. This time his support came from the French-speaking Métis and Indians, notably Crees led by Poundmaker and Big Bear. On 19 March 1885, Riel established a headquarters at the village of Batoche and set up a provisional government. Riel was the civil governor, and his adjutant-general was the experienced buffalo hunter and fine horseman, Gabriel Dumont.

Batoche, May 1885

Batoche was the decisive but not the last battle of the Northwest Rebellion of 1885. Of the encounters between the military and the people of mixed Indian-European ancestry, the Batoche battle ground is the best one to visit.

Because it is in a rural area, little affected by development, the site has become a national historic park of some 1,600 hectares (2,700 acres). The ground lies at a deep bend in the South Sasketchewan River, on Highway 225 in the rural municipality of Duck Lake, three kilometres north of the present spot known as Batoche. On 21 March, Riel called on the NWMP detachment at Fort Carlton to surrender, and on the 26th, Dumont led a band of Métis who ambushed Superintendent Leif N.F. Crozier and ninety-two of his constables at Duck Lake. Crozier lost twelve men killed and Dumont's losses were five dead. Two days later the Mounties evacuated Fort Carlton and withdrew to the white settlement of Prince Albert, downstream. On the 30th, 200 Crees under Poundmaker attacked Battleford and white settlers fled to the NWMP barracks nearby. Then on 2 April, Crees led by Wandering Spirit massacred nine whites at Frog Lake.

By that time telegraphed messages had reached Ottawa, and Macdonald ordered an army to take to the field. The commander of what was called the North West Field Force was sixty-year-old Major-General Frederick Middleton, a British career soldier who had been appointed commander-in-chief of the Canadian militia in November 1884. The army also included a column called the Alberta Field Force that was dispatched to Calgary with orders to march north to Edmonton.

This force, commanded by Major-General Thomas B. Strange, comprised a detachment of NWMP under Major Samuel B. Steele, the 65th Mount Royal Rifles from Montreal, and the Winnipeg Light Infantry, in all 57 officers and 600 men.

Two columns made up the North West Field Force, one under Middleton, the other led by Lieutenant-Colonel William D. Otter. In Otter's column were 'B' Battery, Regiment of Canadian Artillery from Kingston, a detachment of NWMP from the garrisons of Fort Pitt and Battleford, the Queen's Own Rifles of Toronto, part of 'C' Company from the Infantry School Corps of Toronto, some Gevernor-General's Foot Guards sharpshooters from Ottawa, and the Battleford Rifles — a combined strength of 34 officers and 550

The Northwest Rebellion 1885

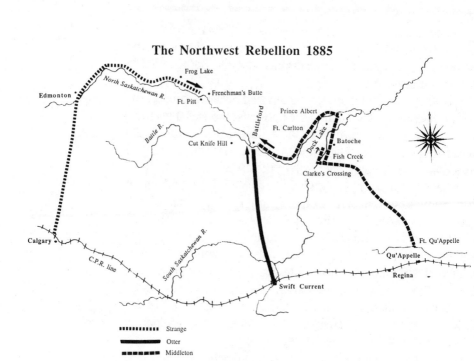

Strange ....

Otter ▬▬▬▬

Middleton ▪ ▪ ▪ ▪ ▪ ▪ ▪

Scale

| 0 | 50 | 100 | Miles |

| 0 | 80 | 100 | Kilometres |

The C.P.R. line played a vital role in moving troops into the Northwest, even though it was not fully built, with gaps in the vicinity of Lake-of-the-Woods. The difficult marching commenced from the three points along the railway where the troops disembarked.

men.

Middleton's column fought the Battle of Batoche. This force was made up of 'A' Battery, Regiment of Canadian Artillery from Quebec (Lieutenant-Colonel C.E. Montizambert), the Winnipeg Field Battery (Major E.W. Jarvis), a detachment of 'C' Company, Infantry School Corps of Toronto (Major Henry Smith), the 10th Royal Grenadiers of Toronto (Lieutenant-Colonel H.J. Grasett), the 90th Battalion of Rifles from Winnipeg (Lieutenant-Colonel Alfred Mackeand), mounted infantry from Russel and Birtle, Manitoba (Major Charles A. Boulton), and scouts from Qu'Appelle (Captain John French).

Headquarters for Otter's column were at Swift Current, and for Middleton at Qu'Appelle. All the troops were transported by rail where track existed. Some gaps had yet to be filled along the north shore of Lake Superior and Lake of the Woods.

General (later Sir Frederick) Middleton, commander of the North West Field Force in 1885. Middleton was considered competent but not brilliant.

Middleton's column reached Qu'Appelle on 6 April and set out to march towards Batoche, the seat of Riel's government. On the 13th, Otter's column left from Swift Current and marched for Saskatchewan Landing on the South Saskatchewan River, where the Hudson's Bay Company steamer *Northcote* would take the men on to Battleford to disperse Poundmaker's Crees. The steamer was to return with all dispatch to carry supplies for Middleton's column as far as Clarke's Crossing, south of Fish Creek on the South Saskatchewan.

On the 15th, Inspector Francis Dickens (son of the author Charles Dickens) withdrew the NWMP detachment from Fort Pitt because it was being menaced by Big Bear and some of his Crees, and he reached Battleford on the 22nd. On the 24th, Otter arrived at Battleford and on the same day Middleton's column was attacked by Gabriel Dumont at Fish Creek, on the South Saskatchewan River above Batoche.

The encounter badly unnerved Middleton, for his casualties were eleven killed and forty-eight wounded.

On 2 May, Otter attacked Poundmaker and his Crees at Cut Knife Hill, near Battleford, and he withdrew after eight of his men had been killed and fifteen wounded. That same day Strange reached Edmonton. The next episode was the Battle of Batoche. Middleton was a conservative man who placed his confidence in his infantry, but the situation called for cavalry and mobility. Beyond the railway lines, the conditions of travel did not favour an army on the march. Creeks had to be crossed, the roads were poor, and ferries were often out of action. Hay and fodder for the horses took up most of the space on Middleton's wagons.

The steamer *Northcote* left Saskatchewan Landing on 23 April, carrying food, hay and oats, part of a field hospital and two companies of the Midland Battalion, from Belleville, Lindsay, Port Hope and Kingston, under the command of the Lieutenant-Colonel, Arthur Williams M.P., and one of two Gatling guns which the government had purchased. Middleton waited for the *Northcote* in his encampment at Fish Creek until 2 May. Then he sent some of Boulton's horsemen to reconnoitre the land surrounding Batoche. The *Northcote* finally appeared on the 5th, and Middleton had the steamer fortified with large boards. He planned a two-pronged attack on Batoche, one from the steamer, the other by

Midnight tramp of the 10th Royal Grenadiers en route to the Northwest. Part of the way the volunteers travelled by rail, but where gaps existed they had to march or use boats.

The 90th Battalion of Rifles leaving Winnipeg for the front. From The Illustrated War News, *Toronto, 11 April 1885.*

land. The *Northcote* was to descend the river from Fish Creek and attack at the same time as the land force that would move on Batoche from the south. Aboard the steamer Middleton placed Major Henry Smith and 'C' Company of the Infantry School Corps. The two companies of the Midland Battalion that had arrived on the steamer would replace Smith's force and the casualties of Fish Creek

On 7 May, Middleton left Fish Creek with his 850 men, four 9-pounder guns, the Gatling gun which was in charge of Arthur Howard, a former United States Army captain, and fifty wagons. Lieutenant-Colonel Bowen Van Straubenzie, a former regular officer, was in command of the infantry. The expedition followed the river to Gabriel's Crossing, then swung inland and camped some ten kilometres south of the village. The *Northcote* was under orders to attack Batoche at 9.00 a.m. on the 9th, a Saturday.

The Métis had fortified their village with well-placed rifle pits — trenches with log barricades concealed with brush — which covered many parts of the site. From the river bend the ground was high at the southwest end, with shore bluffs, and lower to north and east. A cemetery, church and seminary stood on the higher ground. The village was north again on both sides of a large ravine

The church at Batoche, Batoche National Historic Park. The early stages of the battle took place around the church.

which led down to a cable ferry. Batoche was better protected by natural factors to south and west than to east and north, where it lay open to the prairie. The Carlton Trail, the main trade route, lay through the cluster of houses to the ferry. The houses sat in a depression to the east of the ferry.

The rifle pits had been dug on slopes facing downward away from the village on its three landward sides. Riel's headquarters were in the home of Xavier Letendre *dit* Batoche, who had started the ferry and who operated a store.

Prisoners the Métis had captured were confined in the store. Indian supporters who had come to help the Métis were encamped along the more gently sloping part of the river bank to the north of the main cluster of houses. About 500 people lived in the settlement, and Dumont's force amounted to 300 Métis and Indians.

During 8 May, Middleton's expedition moved to within two kilometres of Batoche and camped for the night. At 6.00 a.m. on the 9th, the camp was stirring and the men began preparing to march to attack the Métis rifle pits on the south side of the village at 9.00 a.m., to coordinate with the attack by the steamer *Northcote*. Then, to Middleton's annoyance, sounds of battle could be heard coming from the river at 8.00 a.m., an hour too early. The *Northcote* had been spotted by Dumont, and a brisk exchange of rifle fire followed. The Métis had raised the ferry cable, which shreered off the steamer's funnels and mast, but that did not stop her. The Métis had raised the cable too high and the hull of *Northcote* was able to slip beneath it. Major Smith asked the captain to turn back but he declined. He was an American who saw no need to endanger himself in a 'foreign' quarrel. Smith appointed a substitute but the crew refused to serve under him and the steamer continued to Prince Albert.

Middleton's column advanced towards the Métis rifle pits, moved from marching formation into battle line and extended, the 10th Royal Grenadiers on the right as they faced Batoche. The 90th Rifles were on the left, lining the river bank and trying to prevent any Métis slipping along the wooded slope and gaining their rear. Scouts and the Gatling gun were on the right beyond the Grenadiers, to prevent outflanking from that direction. The Métis in their rifle pits were still largely invisible. Middleton's men advanced to the vicinity of the church and found a white flag flying over a house nearby, where three priests, some nuns and some women and children had taken shelter.

When the firing began, it was especially heavy on the troops close to Mission Ridge, between the river bank and the church. At that point Middleton was afraid that his inexperienced militia were

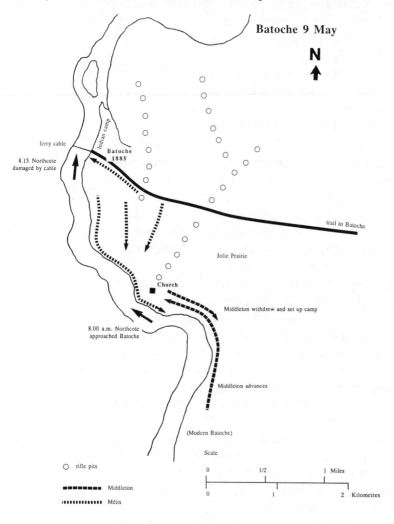

Movements of the Métis and the troops on the first day of the battle. Little happened on the second day, 10 May.

not capable of an orderly retreat, and they could only advance with heavy losses. He had Major Boulton take some of his mounted infantry and bring the wagon train from the camp of the night before closer to the Métis entrenchments. On the farm of John Caron Sr., Boulton formed the wagons into a square which was the first stage in building what Middleton called the zareba. In the afternoon, while the troops remained around the church, Middleton sent his chief of staff, Lord Melgund, to Humboldt ostensibly to telegraph messages to Ottawa. Middleton wanted Melgund out of the way. If the Métis were to defeat his force, Melgund would be the man to lead a relief expedition and Middleton did not want to risk losing him.

That night of 9 May, at dusk, Middleton called his men back and they camped on the Caron farm inside their wagon square. Not much happened on Sunday 10 May.

Middleton had his men take up the position around the church, skirmish, and withdraw into the zareba for the night. Other troops dug trenches to make the encampment secure. Middleton had Captain John French lead a small party to find some open plain for a better approach to Batoche. French favoured the piece of open grassland known as Jolie Prairie, and reported it to Middleton. Before the day was out, fifty Land Surveyors — volunteers who had organized themselves into a company led by Captain John S. Dennis, Jr. (his father was one of the commanders of the Ridgeway raid)— arrived in camp.

On the morning of Monday 11 May, the infantrymen again marched to positions around the church for more skirmishing, with a few casualties. Middleton led a party to Jolie Prairie to see that spot, and was pleased. He had a clear view all the way to the river. When the Métis learned of his presence they suspected an attack from that direction and hurried to reinforce the rifle pits on the north and east of Batoche.

Middleton felt that he had enough men to hold his position, but not enough to capture the village. He sent a messenger to telegraph his plight to Ottawa.

All troops then in the Northwest were ordered to Batoche. These were Lieutenant-Colonel W.E. O'Brien's York and Simcoe Rangers, George Taylor Denison's troop of horse from Toronto, and men of the 7th Fusiliers of London who were trying to bring barges of supplies from Saskatchewan Landing to Fish Creek, and the rest of the Midland Battalion.

Early on the 12th, while the troops were again moving to their positions near the church, Riel sent two prisoners to Middleton to inform him that if he massacred Métis women and children by continuing to shell the houses in the village, he would have no choice

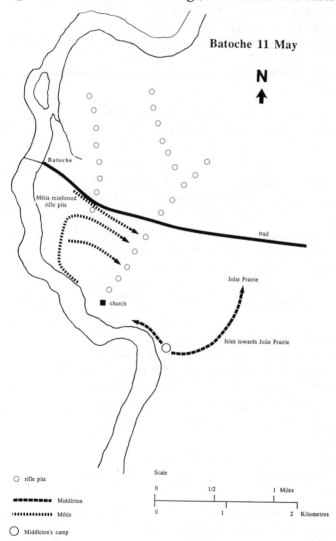

Actions on the third day of the battle for Batoche from Middleton's camp.

but to kill all his prisoners. One of the prisoner-emissaries, John Astley, a surveyor, agreed to return to Riel with Middleton's reply, which was that if Riel would place all women and children together and raise a white flag, the troops would respect it. The other prisoner, Thomas Jackson, refused to return, preferring to break his parole to Riel.

Middleton's troops were wearying of his uninspired leadership, and of the routine of advance, skirmish and retire for the night. The Métis, too, were tired of the standoff and they had never considered that a long siege might occur. By now they were short of ammunition.

Now Middleton tried a new approach, again a two-pronged attack. Part of his force would move to Jolie Prairie, and the rest would continue in the usual position near the church. A detachment of artillery moved to Jolie Prairie, directly under the command of Middleton, Lieutenant-Colonel Van Straubenzie was in command of the infantry around the church. Upon hearing gunfire from Jolie Prairie, Van Straubenzie was to advance, the idea being that the gunfire from Jolie Prairie would draw off some of the Métis facing the infantry position.

The gun fired, and it attracted some of the Métis, but Van Straubenzie's infantry did not move. Middleton hurried back, furious, to enquire why. Van Straubenzie had not heard the gunfire because he was upwind of Jolie Prairie and the sound did not carry.

The companies of the Midland Battalion under Lieutenant-Colonel Williams were on the left closest to the river. On their right was the 90th Battalion under Lieutenant-Colonel Alfred Mackeand, and on the right end of the line the 10th Royal Grenadiers under Lieutenant-Colonel H.J. Grasett. Beyond, towards Jolie Prairie, were scouts from the Surveyors and from Boulton's group. The troops, and many of their officers, were now ready to take matters into their own hands.

Williams and Grasett in particular were determined not to be pulled back as on the three previous days. The men of the Midland Battalion set off, on Middleton's orders, to move between the cemetery and the river bank, until the men were close to the forward part of the line. As the Midlanders advanced, so did the rest of the line, the troops racing upslope through the rifle pits and downhill towards Batoche, shouting. Middleton could no longer control them, and the troops at either end extended to prevent out-flanking movements by the Métis.

Dumont was an easy prey. His force of defenders had been so reduced by desertion that it numbered only ninety men, and he was taken by surprise. He had also moved some men from the rifle pits

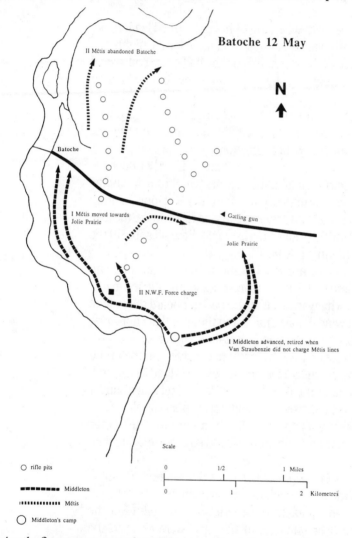

Batoche 12 May

II Métis abandoned Batoche

N

Batoche

I Métis moved towards Jolie Prairie

Gatling gun

Jolie Prairie

II N.W.F. Force charge

I Middleton advanced, retired when Van Straubenzie did not charge Métis lines

Scale

○ rifle pits

■■■■■■■ Middleton

🔴🔴🔴🔴 Métis

◯ Middleton's camp

| 0 | 1/2 | 1 Miles |
| 0 | 1 | 2 Kilometres |

During the first stage on 12 May, Middleton moved to Jolie Prairie. The Métis moved towards Middleton. Next, when Van Straubenzie did not advance, Middleton returned to his camp. Finally the North West Field Force charged Batoche and the Métis withdrew northwards.

238

in front of the infantrymen to guard against attack from Jolie Prairie. As the guns and ammunition of 'A' Battery and the Winnipeg Field Battery were rushed foward, the Métis began abandoning their rifle pits, and soon Dumont's force was fleeing north. The few who stayed were killed. The only effective fire was from houses in the village. Late in the afternoon Middleton realized that his troops were in control of Batoche and the Métis defenders had gone. He summed up his losses as four officers and one other rank killed, and twenty-five wounded. His men found twenty-one dead Métis and five wounded, but one of the priests informed him that fifty-one Métis and Indians had been killed, and all but four of them died on 12 May.

At 6.00 p.m. a steamboat whistle sounded, and the *Northcote*, last seen heading for Prince Albert on Saturday 9 May, three days earlier, hove into view, towing the steamboat *Marquis*. After the crew of the *Northcote* had insisted on going to Prince Albert, Major Henry Smith disembarked and went to the Hudson's Bay Company ferry, where he and found the *Marquis*, guarded by some Mounties. Smith had set out for Batoche with the *Northcote* and the *Marquis*, and when the latter developed a problem in her steering gear the *Northcote* took her in tow.

Middleton sent out messengers to inform Riel that he would protect him until the government decided what to do about him. On 15 May Riel surrendered to two of Boulton's scouts who found him near the main trail. He was on his way to find Middleton. Yet the rebellion was not quite over.

On 23 May, Poundmaker with his Indians and 150 Métis surrendered to Middleton at Battleford. On the 28th, General Strange attacked Big Bear and his Crees at Frenchman's Butte, but Big Bear escaped. Frenchman's Butte is notable because it is Alberta's only battle ground. The last military engagement of the 1885 rebellion, and incidently the last on Canadian soil, occurred when a party of NWMP led by Major Samuel Steele clashed with Big Bear and his Crees at Steele Narrows, Saskatchewan, on 3 June. Big Bear again eluded the soldiers and police. Not until 2 July did he surrender. Poundmaker and Big Bear were imprisoned for two years for their part in the uprisings. Wandering Spirit and seven other Indians were hanged for murder at Fort Battleford on 27 November.

By that time Louis Riel was dead, hanged at Regina jail on the

16th. He was executed not for his part in the rebellions, but for the execution of Thomas Scott on 4 March 1870. That act had far-reaching consequences. Scott had become a martyr for Ontario, although by all accounts he was a nasty character.

Louis Riel became Quebec's martyr, where his highly independent views on religion were overlooked and he was remodelled into a champion of French Canada.

The execution of Louis Riel angered Quebec voters and turned them away from the Conservative Party. As a result the Liberal

The execution of Louis Riel. The Métis leader was hanged in Regina on 16 November 1885.

Party has been able to operate from a firm Quebec base almost continually over since.

The Métis suffered but they were not destroyed as a result of the rebellions. Many moved farther north to avoid the white settlers, and some were able to remain in their communities, growing a few crops and raising livestock once the buffalo were gone. Some settlements were looted; one officer reported that soldiers stole furs they found in Batoche. Some Métis property was burned, yet Batoche remained a Métis community for a while, bypassed by the railway lines and main roads. Gradually the Métis drifted away, some to assimilate with the white population, others to eke out livings in various ways, a minority that others could ignore.

Making a stand at Batoche was probably Riel's idea, not Dumont's. The Métis put up a good defence from their rifle pits, but that was not their style of fighting. Had they ridden away and employed hit and run tactics against Middleton's unwieldy column, they could have kept on indefinitely. Perhaps it was as well that the rebellion was blunted at Batoche. Otherwise Macdonald would have authorized more troops. More damage would have been done, thereby arousing stronger demands for revenge on Riel's people.

Afterwards

Canada is one of the most fortunate of countries in that she has not had a battle on home ground for more than a century. That does not mean that Canadian soldiers have stopped going to battle, far from it. Canadian soldiers were fighting overseas as early as 1884. These men sailed on 15 September 1884 for Egypt. Led by Colonel Frederick Denison of Toronto, this force of 386 men was composed of Caughnawaga Indians and boatmen. They were part of relief force dispatched to rescue Major-General Charles 'Chinese' Gordon, who was besieged at Khartoum, in the Sudan, by revolutionaries led by the Mahdi. The relief force was commanded by Field-Marshal Lord Wolseley, who had led the expedition against Riel's rebels at Red River in 1870. Wolseley had been so impressed with the efficiency of the *voyageurs* that he obtained permission from Ottawa to use them to help ascend the Nile. The *voyageurs* − apparently in their birchbark canoes − led the British up the river, finding the Nile cataracts much more challenging that the white waters of Lake-of-the-Woods. Wolseley's force reached Khartoum on 28 January 1885, by which time the city had fallen to the Mahdi and Gordon was dead. Sixteen Canadians died during the campaign, and the rest returned to Quebec on 25 May 1885.

The Boer War marked the second occasion when a Canadian expeditionary force was sent overseas, likewise to Africa. Two of the leaders in the suppression of the 1885 Rebellion led contingents that departed for service in South Africa's Boer War. The first − 57 officers and 1,224 men of the second battalion, Royal Canadian Regiment − left Quebec on 30 October 1899, under the command of Colonel William Otter, who was in charge of the troops that fought the Battle of Cut Knife Hill, Saskatchewan.

Otter's infantry regiment was followed on 2 November by 1,281 men of mounted rifle and artillery units. Then on 16 February it was the turn of 537 mounted men of Lord Strathcona's Horse, raised in Manitoba, to sail away. The commander of Strathcona's Horse was Samuel Steele, who had led the North West Mounted Police on 3 June 1885 at the last battle on Canadian soil. By the time the war ended, on 31 May 1902, some 7,400 Canadians had served, and 242 had died while on active service.

During World War I (1914-1918), of 628,642 people who joined the Canadian armed forces, 424,589 went overseas. The war dead numbered 60,661, and thousands more were left crippled or otherwise disabled. The death toll was less in World War II (1939-1945). Of 1,086,771 Canadians who served (49,252 of them were women), 41,992 gave up their lives. The Korean War lasted from June 1950 untli July 1953. A naval contingent and some of Canada's most famous regiments joined the United Nations force — among them the Royal 22nd, the Princess Patricia's Canadian Light Infantry, and the Royal Canadian Regiment. Of 26,665 military and naval personnel sent to Korea, 314 sacrificed their lives.

At the time of the Korean War, the 27th Canadian Infantry Brigade Group was formed for service with NATO in Europe. The first units arrived in Hanover, Germany on 15 November 1951.

A country of vast size but small population, Canada has always depended on a much stronger power for security. In the nineteenth century that power was Britain, whose professional soldiers, even when numbers were hardly adequate, helped preserve Canadian sovereignty. In the time of uncertainty now facing the world, Canada again relies on a protector. Whether the new arrangement will serve as well as the old is one of the questions whose answers lie in the future.

Chronology of Important Dates
in the Military History of Canada

875-1,000
Beginning of European interest in North America.
1004
Norse founded a camp at l'Anse aux Meadows, Newfoundland, and abandoned it two years later.
1390
Formation of the Iroquois Confederacy by Dekanawidah and his assistant Adodaroh (Hiawatha) uniting the Mohawks, Oneidas, Onondagas, Cayugas and Senecas into the Five Nations. (In 1722 the Tuscaroras joined, making the Six Nations.)
ca. 1420
Basque Whalers from France and Spain began to hunt in the Labrador Sea.
1481
British ''Merchants of Bristowe'' may have landed in Newfoundland, but they kept their activities secret to avoid competition from the French, Spanish and Portugese on the Grand Banks.
1494
Treaty of Tordesillas gave the Americas to Spain, who was too busy in the Caribbean and South America to notice the British and French in Newfoundland waters.
1504
St. John's Nfld. was established.
1506
A Norman fishing village was established on the east side of the Avalon Peninsula, Nfld.
1534
Jacques Cartier planted a cross on the Gaspé Peninsula, on the first of three voyages of exploration he made for France.
1576
26 August. British explorer Martin Frobisher claimed the land around Frobisher Bay for Britain.
1587
The Marquis de la Roche-Mesgoues was appointed the first Viceroy of New France by Henry IV of France.

1583
5 August. Humphrey Gilbert claimed Newfoundland for Elizabeth I of England.
1605
Founding of Port Royal (Nova Scotia) by Pierre du Gua, Sieur de Monts, and Samuel de Champlain, first capital of Acadia.
1608
Founding of Quebec by merchants led by Champlain.
1609
30 July. Champlain and his men defeated an Iroquois war party near Ticonderoga, Lake Champlain
1610
14-19 June. Champlain and his Huron and Algonquin allies defeated the Iroquois near the mouth of the Richelieu River.
1610-1611
Henry Hudson in his ship *Discovery* wintered in James Bay. Champlain sent Etienne Brulé to winter among the Hurons.
1612
Peter Easton used Harbour Grace, Nfld. as a base for his ten-vessel pirate fleet that plundered thirty English ships in St. John's harbour and raided French and Portugese ships at Ferryland.
1613
July. Port Royal was attacked, sacked and burnt by Capt. Samuel Argall, on orders from Sir Thomas Dale, Governor of Virginia, the first British expedition against Acadia.
Beverwyck (Albany, N.Y.) was founded as a trading post by the Dutch.
Récollet Father Joseph Le Caron reached Huronia (and returned to Quebec in 1616).
3 August. Champlain arrived in Huronia.
1 September-23 December. Champlain joined the Hurons for an expedition against the Iroquois. On 10 October. the Onondogas ambushed them, Champlain was wounded, and the French and Hurons retired to Huronia.
1616
17 June. William Vaughan founded a Welsh

colony at Trepassey Bay, Nfld.
1620
Late July Champlain began construction of Fort St. Louis on Cape Diamond, the first fort on the cliff at Quebec.
1621
The Iroquois began getting firearms from the Dutch.
10 September. James I granted land from Cape Gaspé to the St. Croix River to the Scotsman, William Alexander, despite French claims.
1622
July. The first Scots colonists reached Nova Scotia.
1624
Three Récollets founded a mission in Huronia (which was taken over by the Jesuits in 1626).
Temporary peace reigned between the French, Hurons and Algonquins and the Iroquois.
1625
19 June. First Jesuits reached Quebec.
1626
July. Jesuit Father Jean de Brébeuf founded a mission in Huronia (on the site of Penatanguishene).
1627
Britain and France were at war.
1629
19 July. Quebec was captured by Capt. David Kirke. Champlain and all the missionaries were sent to France.
1632
29 March. Quebec and Port Royal were restored to France by the Treaty of St.-Germain-en-Laye.
1633
22 May. Champlain and four Jesuit priests reached Quebec. The missionaries returned to Huronia in 1634.
1639
Jesuit Father Jérôme Lalemant founded Ste.-Marie-Among-the-Hurons (near Midland, Ont.).
1641

The Iroquois formally declared war on the French.
1642
August. The French built Fort Richelieu as protection for Montreal.
1642-1649 Destruction of Huronia
2 August. Jesuits Isaac Joques and René Goupil, en route to Quebec, were captured by Iroquois near Trois Rivières. Goupil was killed, the first Jesuit Martyr, and Joques escaped.
1644
30 March. Settlers were defeated by a large band of Iroquois intent on attacking Montreal.
1645
April. Attack on Fort Ste. Marie, stronghold of Acadian Charles de la Tour by his Acadian rival, Menou d'Aulnay. On the 13th, the 45 defenders surrendered, and most were hanged.
14 July. A peace was arranged between the Iroquois and French.
1646
September-October. Fathers Isaac Joques and lay brother Jean de La Lande were killed while on a peace mission to the Mohawks.
1648
Summer. Iroquois broke the peace by attacking the Jesuit missions of St. Joseph II and St. Michel in Huronia. Father Antoine Daniel was killed.
1649
16 March. A force of 1,000 Iroquois attacked St. Ignace and St. Louis missions. Fathers Jean de Brébeuf and Gabriel Lalemant were tortured to death.
14 June. The Jesuits abandoned Ste.-Marie among-the Hurons and moved to Christian Island to found Ste.-Marie II.
1650
Spring. Father Paul Ragueneau evacuated Ste.-Marie-II and returned to Quebec.
1653
Iroquois made a general peace with the French.

1654

3 July. Major Robert Sedgewick, commander on the New England coast, left Boston and attacked Acadia in reprisal for French attacks on British vessels. He captured Fort Ste. Marie, Port Royal and Fort Penobscot.

1655

3 November. By the Treaty of Westminster, Acadia was restored to France.

1660

May. Battle of the Long Sault of the Ottawa River (near the site of Hawkesbury). It was fought between 16 French and 44 Indian allies and some 800 Iroquois. All the French died.

1660

The French founded Plaisance, at Placentia Bay, Nfld.

1665

30 June. Alexandre de Tracy arrived in Quebec with 100 officers and 1,000 men of the Carnignan-Salières Regiment. The soldiers built a chain of forts along the Richelieu River.

1666

9 January-17 March. Sieur de Courcelle, Governor of New France, attacked the Mohawks. Of 500 French, 60 died of hunger and exposure.

14 September-5 November. Courcelle led a second expedition, of 1,500 men against the Mohawks. He burned many villages and claimed the land for Louis XIV of France.

1669

Voyage of the Nonsuch to Hudson Bay. Médard Chouard des Groseilliers established Charles Fort and returned to England with a cargo of furs.

1670

2 May. Charles II granted a charter to his cousin Prince Rupert and his associates as the ''Governor and Company of Adventurers Trading into Hudson's Bay''. Radisson and Groseilliers sailed with the first governor of the Hudson's Bay

Company, Charles Bayly.

1671

2 June. Governor de Courcelle left Montreal and met with Iroquois leaders on Lake Ontario, who agreed to make peace.

1673

13 June. Robert Cavelier de La Salle began building Fort Frontenac (on the site of Kingston, Ont.).

17 July. The Dutch attacked Ferryland, Nfld.

August. The Dutch retook New York (New Amsterdam) from the British.

1674

9 February. By the Treaty of Westminster the Dutch restored New York (New Netherlands) colony to Britain.

10 August. Dutch Privateer Jurriaen Aernoutsz, unaware of the peace treaty, captured Penagouet, in Acadia, and took the governor, Jacques de Chambly, prisoner. After plundering French posts along the Bay of Fundy and capturing Jemseg (Saint John), Aernoutsz took his booty to Boston and claimed Acadia for Holland.

1675

The Iroquois attacked tribes friendly to the French.

1682

La Salle reached the Gulf of Mexico in April.

The French, including Radisson and Groseilliers, who had left the Hudson's Bay Company, built a fur post on the Hayes River close to Hudson Bay, captured York Fort on the Nelson River, and set up the *Compagnie du Nord*, to compete with the Hudson's Bay Company.

April. The Iroquois attacked tribes friendly to the French.

1684

York Fort was returned to the Hudson's Bay Company.

5 September. The Governor of New France, Joseph Le Febre de la Barre, with 700 French and 400 Indians, met the Iroquois

French and 400 Indians, met the Iroquois on Lake Ontario, who signed a treaty to keep the peace with the Miamis.

1686

20 March-June. Expedition under Pierre de Troyes and Pierre le Moyne d'Iberville, of 100 men, marched overland to Hudson Bay and seized the Hudson's Bay Company's three forts.

19 November. Britain and France signed the Neutrality Pact to settle the dispute over Hudson Bay. A commission would decide on the boundary between New France and Rupert's Land.

1687

17 June. Governor Jacques Denonville and De Troyes left Montreal with an expedition against the Senecas. Denonville left De Troyes and a garrison to build Fort Niagara on Seneca land.

1688

15 September. Because of Iroquois demands, Denonville ordered Fort Niagara demolished and abandoned.

1689

28 January. A French force left Trois Rivières to attack New England settlements.

1689-1697 King William's War

17 May. War was declared between Britain and France.

5 August. 1,500 Iroquois attacked Lachine, the worst disaster in the history of New France; 24 were killed, and 42 of 90 who were captured were never seen again.

October. Fort Frontenac was abandoned. Iberville surrendered Fort New Severn, on Hudson Bay, and he defended Fort Albany successfully.

13 November. La Chènage (near Montreal) was attacked by Iroquois and some settlers were massacred.

1690

22 January. At Onondaga, the Iroquois agreed to a peace treaty between England and the tribes of the Great Lakes.

8 February. Governor Frontenac organized war parties to attack British frontier settlements.

18 February. French and Indians led by Jacques Le Moyne and Nicolas D'Ailleboust de Manthet raided Schenectady, N.Y., massacred 60 inhabitants, and returned to Montreal with 50 horses laden with plunder.

18 March. The French, led by François Hertel de Rouville, attacked Salmon Falls, on the New Hampshire frontier, killed 34 and took 54 prisoner, burned buildings and slaughtered livestock.

19 May. William Phips, Provost-Marshal of New England, took a naval force to Port Royal, which surrendered on the 21st.

July. Iberville entered Hudson Bay with three small ships, raided Fort New Severn, and with booty returned to Quebec in October. 1691.

16 October. Phips was off Quebec with 37 ships and 2,200 men. Frontenac, who had 3,000 troops, refused to surrender, and Phips sailed away after some skirmishes.

1692

A British attack on Placentia was repulsed.

Governor Joseph de Villebon built Fort St. Joseph farther up the Saint John River (N.B.).

The Hudson's Bay Company rebuilt Fort Nelson and recaptured Fort Albany.

5 February. Abenakis massacred some British at York, Me.

22 October. Fourteen-year-old Madeleine de Verchères led a successful defence of the family fort against attacking Iroquois.

Autumn. Iberville, preying upon New England shipping, planned to plunder settlements, but found them too well guarded. He led two frigates and captured three prize ships before sailing for France in November.

1693

28 January. A force of Caughnawagas led by Nicolas d'Ailleboust de Manthet

attacked the Mohawk villages and captured 300 before a relief force under Peter Schuyler forced the French to withdraw.

The British retook Albany Fort and drove the French from Hudson Bay.

1694

16 January. French missionaries Louis-Pierre Thury and Sébastien de Billie led 230 Indians in an attack on Oyster Bay, Me., killing 100 settlers.

31 August. Seven French vessels were defeated by the English ships *William* and *Mary* off Ferryland, Nfld.

15 October. Iberville captured York Fort and renamed it Fort Bourbon. A new fur post was opened by the French at Michilimackinac by Antoine de Lamothe Cadillac.

1695

July. Frontenac sent Thomas Crisafy and 700 men to restore Fort Frontenac.

Autumn. Iberville sailed for France, where he received orders to attack British settlements on the Atlantic coast.

1696

A French campaign against Britain's coastal colonies began.

4 July. Frontenac left Montreal with 2,150 men to punish the Iroquois for attacks on French settlements.

14 July. Iberville and Simon de Bonaventure, a naval officer, captured the British ship *Newport* near St. John's.

August. Iberville reached the mouth of the Saint John River, lifted a British blockade that entrapped Governor Joseph de Villebon of Acadia, and captured a British frigate.

15 August. Iberville captured Fort William Henry, Me. from Capt. Pascoe Chubb, 25 Acadia-based British regulars and 240 Abenakis. Iberville sent 90 prisoners to Boston and sailed for Placentia 28 August. Capt. William Allen captured York Fort from the French.

Autumn. The French Governor of Placentia, Jacques de Brouillon, with Iberville, set out to expel the British from Newfoundland.

November. Iberville marched across the Avalon Peninsula, destroyed Ferryland, and captured St. John's on the 30th. Looting and burning continued until only Carbonear and Bonavista remained in British hands, when Iberville was ordered to Hudson Bay. Thirty-six settlements had been wrecked, 200 people killed.

1697

Spring. A British squadron and 200 soldiers under Sir John Gibson arrived at St. John's to serve as a garrison.

5-13 September. In Hudson Bay, Iberville with 5 ships defeated 3 British ships and captured York Fort.

20 September. The Treaty of Ryswick ended King William's War. Newfoundland and Hudson Bay were ceded to Britain, and Acadia to France.

1700

8 September. Iroquois, Abenakis and Ottawas agreed to peace terms with the governor of New France, Louis de Callières.

1701

July. Detroit was founded by Cadillac and his lieutenant, Alphonse Tonty.

1702

1702-1713 Queen Anne's War (part of the War of the Spanish Succession).

15 May. England declared war on France.

1704

28 February. The French and Indians raided Deerfield, Mass., the worst of several led by Jean-Baptiste Hertel de Rouville; 54 settlers were killed and 120 taken prisoner.

20 June. Benjamin Church captured Les Mines (Grand Pré), Pipigiguit, Cobequid (Truro, N.S.) and Beaubassin at the head of Chignecto Bay, in retaliation for the Deerfield raid.

18 August. French and Indians destroyed the English settlement at Bonavista, Nfld.

the English settlement at Bonavista, Nfld.

1705

8 January. Daniel de Subercase, Governor of Placentia, Nfld., with 450 French troops, captured Bay Bulls, Petty Harbour, and the settlements at Conception and Trinity Bays, except for Carbonear.

1707

6 June. A British attack on Port Royal was repelled by Subercase, recently appointed Governor of Acadia.

20 August. A second British attack on Port Royal by John March leading Massachusetts militia was also repelled by Subercase.

1708

Militia at St. John's formed the Royal Newfoundland Regiment.

26 July. Hertel de Rouville and Jean-Baptiste Deschaillons left Montreal to attack Haverhill, Mass. They killed 15 British settlers, and lost 10 killed and 19 wounded.

14 December. Philippe de Costebelle, Governor of Placentia, and Joseph de Brouillon left Placentia to attack St. John's, which surrendered on 1 January 1709.

1709

July-November. A naval force from Boston under Samuel Vetch and a land force led by Francis Nicholson, prepared to attack Quebec. In October Britain cancelled the naval orders and Vetch did not sail. Nicholson withdrew after skirmishing with the French near Lake Champlain.

1710

29 September. Conquest of Acadia began. An expedition led by Francis Nicholson, a colonial naval force under Samuel Vetch, and a British squadron under Capt. George Martin, sailed from Boston against Port Royal. The French commander, Subercase, surrendered on 1 October. Port Royal became Annapolis Royal.

Simultaneously, a British fleet under Sir Hovenden Walker failed to capture the French settlement at Placentia Bay.

Winter. 80 British soldiers foraging outside Port Royal were massacred by Indians loyal to the French.

1711

July-September. An expedition under Sir Hovenden Walker failed to reach Quebec. In fog, his 9 vessels grounded on shoals in the Gulf of St. Lawrence, with the loss of 8 ships and 900 men, an episode called the "magnificent fiasco".

1713

11 April. The Treaty of Utrecht was signed. Acadia, Newfoundland and the shores of Hudson Bay, were ceded to Britain. France retained New France (Quebec), Ile St. Jean (P.E.I.), and Ile Royal (Cape Breton Island), and the right to fish and use parts of the Newfoundland shore.

August. The French planned a great new fortress at Havre à l'Anglois (Louisbourg).

1714

1 June. Governor Philippe de Costebelle surrendered Placentia to a British force under Capt. John Moody and moved to Ile Royale.

5 September. James Knight, Governor of Hudson Bay lands, and Henry Kelsey, arrived at York Fort to accept the surrender of all the Hudson Bay territories held by the French.

1715

27 June. William Stuart set out from York Fort to bring peace between the Crees and the Chipewyans. He achieved a truce by promising to build a fur fort at the mouth of the Churchill River.

1716

Louis de Louvigny with 400 Indians and 400 *coureurs de bois* defeated the Foxe Indians at Green Bay (Wisc.).

1719

7 March. The contract to build Louisbourg "the Gibralter of Canada" was awarded to Michel Isabeau. Director of fortifications was Jean de Verville, who recommended the site in 1716.

the site in 1716.

1720

British and Dutch traders opened a post a Oswego to deflect furs from the French posts.

1722

July. The French gave ammunition and aid to the Abenakis, who attacked the British settlement of Merrymeeting Bay, Mass. in retaliation for a British attack on the Abenaki village of Norridgewock.

September. 400 Noridgewocks, Hurons of Lorette and Abenakis destroyed British settlements along the lower Kennebec and Connecticut Valleys.

1726

The French established a permanent garrison at Niagara to check British and Dutch competition from Oswego.

1731

1731-1743 Pierre de La Vérendrye and his three sons built a chain of fur posts and explored as far west as the Red River.

1731

The French built Fort St. Frederic at Crown Point, Lake Champlain.

1736

8 June. Jean-Baptiste de La Vérendrye and 20 others were massacred on an island in Lake-of-the Woods by Sioux warriors.

1744

1744-1748 King George's War (War of the Austrian Succession)

15 March. France declared war on Britain.

3 May. Jean Duqesnel, commandant of Cape Breton, sent an expedition under Joseph Du Pont Duvivier against the British fishing station at Canso, which surrendered 24 May.

29 July. The French besieged Annapolis Royal, and withdrew on 2 October.

1745

24 March-17 June. Capture of Louisbourg. New Englanders under Gen. William Pepperrell sailed from Boston, and were joined by Admiral Peter Warren, Royal Navy, with sailors, at Canso. Louisbourg

surrendered on 17 June.

20 June. The French settlement at Three Rivers, P.E.I. was destroyed by New Englanders who had come to Louisbourg. Note: The preceding dates for 1745 are according to the Julian Calendar. England did not adopt the Gregorian Calendar of 1582 until 1752. This has led to confusion between English and Continental dates. French sources date the siege of Louisbourg from 6 April to 30 June, with the attack on Prince Edward Island as 3 July. The latter dates were used in the chapter on Louisbourg.

1746

22 June-30 September. The Duc d'Anville left La Rochelle, France, with 54 ships to retake Louisbourg. After severe storms, the fleet sheltered in Chebucto Bay (Halifax) on 10 September. D'Anville died on the 27th and the fleet sailed for France on the 30th.

10 July. Capt. Jean de Ramezay reached Baie Verte, (N.B.) from Quebec with 700 Canadians and Indians, expecting to meet d'Anville.

1747

11 January. Capt. Nicolas de Villiers, Ramezay's 2nd-in-command, with 240 Canadians and 60 Indians, ambushed 500 British under Governor Arthur Noble at Minas (Grand Pré) on 31 January.

1748

18 October. The Treaty of Aix-la-Chapelle ended King George's War. Louisbourg, Prince Edward Island and Cape Breton Island were returned to France. Britain kept Acadia.

1749

The French started an agricultural settlement at Detroit.

9 July. Col. Edward Cornwallis arrived at Chebucto to found Halifax.

1 June. Abbé François Piquet opened a mission at La Présentation (Ogdensburg N.Y.). The French started a shipyard at Pointe au Baril (Maitland, Ont.).

October. Louis La Corne began fortifications at Beauséjour, on the Isthmus of Chignecto, to limit British settlement to peninsular Nova Scotia.

1750

16 April. Cornwalls sent Col. Charles Lawrence with 400 men to Chignecto to establish British authority. They confronted La Corne on the Missaguash River. La Corne burned the village of Beaubassen to prevent the British taking it.

September. Lawrence returned to Chignecto with a strong force, routed Abbé Le Loutre and his Indians and started work on Fort Lawrence. The French began work on Forts Beauséjour and Gaspareau.

1753

The French opened Fort St. Louis near the forks of the Saskatchewan River, completing a chain of posts controlling the headwaters of rivers flowing into Hudson Bay, to intercept furs en route to the Hudson's Bay Company forts.

The Governor of New France, the Marquis Duquesne, sent a military expedition to build a chain of forts from Lake Erie towards the Ohio Valley.

3 September. The Senecas demanded the removal of the French forts from the Ohio country.

11 December. Virginians under Maj. George Washington arrived in the Ohio country to counter the French occupation.

1754

28 May. Washington and the Seneca, Tanaghrisson, fought the Battle of Jumonville against the French led by Joseph de Jumonville. Washington retreated to Great Meadows and built Fort Necessity.

4 July. Battle of Great Meadows. This started the French and Indian War.

1755

2 June. With 2,000 British troops, Col. Robert Monckton landed at the Missaguash River and began besieging Fort Beauséjour. The French commander,

Louis Du Pont Duchambon de Vergor, surrendered on the 4th.

17 June. Fort Gaspereau, at Baie Verte, surrendered to Monckton's force. That day the French abandoned Fort Jemseg (Saint John N.B.), the last French fort in Acadia.

9 July. Battle of the Monongahela. The French under Daniel de Beaujeu, commander at Fort Duquesne, routed a British-American force under Gen. Edward Braddock near Fort Duquesne. Both Beaujeu and Braddock were killed.

28 July. Lieut. Gov. Charles Lawrence received approval of the Nova Scotia Council to deport Acadians who refused to take the oath of allegiance. (Thousands were expelled in September.)

1 September. French troops under the commander-in-chief, Baron Dieskau, operated against British troops under Col. William Johnson, who had attacked Fort St. Frédéric at Crown Point. Johnson also built a fort at the head of Lake George.

8 September. Battle of Lake George. Dieskau and France's Indian allies defeated 1,000 British and colonial troops under William Johnson. Afterwards the French began building Fort Carillon at Ticonderoga.

1756

1756-1763 The Seven Years' War (French and Indian War)

17 May. Britain declared war on France.

5 August. Oswego. The Marquis de Montcalm, commander of French troops, left Fort Frontenac with 3,000 men to attack the British forts at Oswego. The British garrison, under Col. James Mercer, who was killed, surrendered on 14 August. Britain lost control of Lake Ontario.

1757

21 January. The "Battle on Snowshoes". The French defeated Maj. Robert Rogers and his rangers near Ticonderoga.

26 July. Montcalm and the Chevalier de Lévis defeated a British force under

Col. Parker at Sabbath Day Point, Lake George.

3 August. With 6,200 French and Canadians and 1,800 Indians, Montcalm besieged Fort William Henry, defended by Col. George Munro. The fort surrendered on 9 August.

1758

May-July. Siege of Louisbourg. The British expedition left Halifax, the land force under Gen. Jeffrey Amherst, the naval force led by Admiral Edward Boscawen. The 157 ships carrying 27,000 men lay off Louisbourg on 2 June. The French commander, Augustin de Drucour, with 3,500 regulars, 4,000 sailors and militia, surrendered on 26 July.

8 July. Fort Carillon (Ticonderoga). Montcalm with 3,600 men defeated the British under Gen. James Abercromby with 6,000 regulars and 9,000 provincials, at Fort Carillon.

8 August. From Louisbourg, Capt. Andrew Rollo took a force to Ile St. Jean (P.E.I.) built Fort Amherst at Port-la-Joli (Charlottetown) and deported 3,500 Acadians to France.

27 August. With 3,000 men, Col. John Bradstreet took Fort Frontenac.

29 August. Wolfe left Louisbourg to destroy settlements around the Gaspé and at Miramichi.

14 September. Maj. James Grant and 800 British were defeated at Grant's Hill by French from Fort Duquesne.

25 November. Brigadier John Forbes took Fort Duquesne and renamed it Fort Pitt (Pittsburgh, Pa.).

1759

12 January. Wolfe was appointed commander-in-chief of the land force for the expedition against Quebec.

25 June. Gen. Wolfe arrived off Quebec with 8,500 men; the naval force of 168 ships was commanded by Admiral Charles Saunders.

24 July. A French force under François de Lignery, marching to relieve Fort Niagara, was ambushed and defeated by provincials, regulars and Indians under Sir William Johnson. The fort surrendered on the 25th.

26 July. The British occupied Fort Carillon, and on the 31st Fort St. Frédéric, both abandoned by the French.

31 July. Battle of Montmorency. Wolfe's men were repulsed when they landed on the Beauport shore east of Quebec.

7 September. Part of the British fleet moved above Quebec to Cap Rouge.

9 September. Wolfe spotted a landing site at l'Anse au Foulon.

13 September. Battle of the Plains of Abraham. About 4,000 British regulars under Wolfe defeated a like number of French – regulars, militia and Indians. – Wolfe was killed and Montcalm died of wounds.

17 September. Chevalier de Lévis took command of the French army at Pointe aux Trembles and retreated to Montreal. The British army under Brigadier George Townsend entered Quebec on the 19th.

1760

9 February. On orders from Prime Minister William Pitt, Capt. John Byron began destroying the Louisbourg fortifications.

28 April. Battle of Ste. Foy. Lévis and 5,000 French defeated Brigadier James Murray and 3,900 British. Murray withdrew inside Quebec's walls.

16 May. Lévis abandoned the siege of Quebec when the British fleet arrived with reinforcements.

8 July. Battle of the Ristigouche. British ships under Capt. John Byron defeated a French relief force under François d'Angeac – the last naval engagement fought for New France.

16-25 August. Battle of the Thousand Islands. Amherst's army of 10,000 men arrived at Pointe au Baril, close to Fort Lévis, on an island in the St. Lawrence. The 400 French defenders surrendered on

25 August.
Three armies were converging on Montreal
— Amherst's that had assembled at
Oswego, Haviland's from Lake Champlain,
and Murray's from Quebec.
8 September. Vauderuil surrendered
Montreal to Amherst.
29 November. The French at Detroit
surrendered to Maj. Robert Rogers.

1761
14 February. The British occupied
Michilimackinac.

1762
27 June. French troops under Charles
d'Arsac de Ternay captured Fort William,
at St. John's Nfld.
7 September. Col. William Amherst left
Louisbourg with 1,500 troops to retake St.
John's. They landed at Torbay on the 13th
and drove the French back into Fort
William on the 15th. The French
commander, Joseph d'Haussonville,
surrendered on the 18th. This was the last
encounter between Britain and France in
North America.

1763
10 February The Treaty of Paris ended the
Seven Years' War. France ceded all her
North American possessions to Britain,
except St. Pierre and Miquelon, and part of
Louisiana, retaining fishing rights on the
Grand Banks.
May-June. Pontiac's uprising. The Ottawa
chief's warriors captured all the posts west
of Niagara except Detroit.

1764
12 August. Col. John Bradstreet led a force
against the Delaware and Shawnee
Indians. He avoided a fight, and conducted
peace talks at Presqu'lle (Erie Pa.).
1765-1774 The British Parliament passed
a series of ''Intolerable Acts'' that put the
American colonists in a rebellious frame of
mind.

1774
5 September. The 1st Continental Congress
met in Philadelphia to air grievances over
Britain's Intolerable Acts.

1775
May. Capture of Fort Ticonderoga by
American rebels led by Ethan Allen and
Benedict Arnold; capture of Crown Point
by Seth Warner.
9 June. The Governor of Canada, Guy
Carleton, declared martial law and called
for volunteers to augment his force of 800
British regulars.
Summer. The first American Loyalists
came into Quebec Province. Some served
as volunteers under Carleton.
September. The American rebels began a
two-pronged invasion of Canada, one,
under Brigadier Richard Montgomery,
along the Richelieu River, the other, by
Col. Benedict Arnold, down the Chaudière
River directly towards Quebec.
18 October. Montgomery captured Fort
Chambly.
3 November. St. Jean surrendered to
Montgomery after a long siege.
11 November. Carleton evacuated
Montreal, and Montgomery occupied it on
the 12th.
13 November. Arnold reached the Plains of
Abraham and retreated to Pointe aux
Trembles to await the arrival of
Montgomery.
17 November. Charlottetown (P.E.I.) was
captured by American privateers.
5 December. Arnold and Montgomery
began their siege of Quebec.
31 December. The rebel assault on Quebec
was repulsed by Carleton and Col. Allan
Maclean. Montgomery was killed. The
siege continued until the Spring.

1776
26 January. Eustache de Lotbinière, a
Canadian priest, was appointed chaplain
to serve Canadians who joined the
American rebel army.
1 April. 1,124 American Loyalists arrived
in Halifax from Boston. Many had taken
refuge there, and when the British army
left Boston they had to leave, too.

6 May. Arrival of the British fleet to lift the siege of Quebec.

20 May. Battle of the Cedars. A force of 40 regulars under Capt. George Forster, and 200 Indians, defeated 400 American rebels at their outpost to the west of Montreal.

8 June. American rebels were defeated at Trois Rivières by Brigadier Simon Fraser and the 24th Regiment.

18 June. Sir John Johnson reached Montreal with 200 followers from the Mohawk Valley. On the 19th, at Fort Chambly, Carleton gave him a warrant to raise the King's Royal Regiment of New York.

28 June. Battle of Valcour Island. While pursuing the rebels up Lake Champlain, Carleton's fleet defeated ships commanded by Benedict Arnold.

13 October. Carleton defeated an American rebel fleet at Crown Point.

6 November. Americans from Machias, Me. attacked Fort Cumberland, N.S. and were repulsed.

1777

June-October. Gen. John Burgoyne led an army of 9,000 men south from St. jean along Lake Champlain to reach Albany. Col. Barry St. Leger led a smaller force from Oswego through the Mohawk Valley to meet Burgoyne at Albany. Neither got there.

5 July. Burgoyne captured Fort Ticonderoga.

6 August. Battle of Oriskany. Sir John Johnson, John Butler and Joseph Brant led a force of Loyalists and Indians and ambushed reinforcements under Gen. Nicolas Herkimer.

15 September. John Butler received a warrant to raise a regiment of rangers.

17 October. Burgoyne surrendered at Saratoga N.Y. to rebel Gen. Horatio Gates.

1778

February. France signed an alliance with the American rebels and promised military aid.

27 June. Gen. Frederick Haldimand arrived as governor-in-chief of Canada (Quebec).

3 July. John Butler raided Wyoming, Pa.

11 November. John Butler's son Walter led rangers and Indians in an attack on Cherry Valley N.Y.

1779

Impressment into the Royal Navy was made legal in Canadian ports.

17 June. Brigadier Francis McLean founded a fort at Castine, Me. as an outpost for Halifax.

25 July. Francis McLean beat off an American rebel attack.

1781

28 August. Annapolis Royal was raided by American privateers.

18 October A British army under Lord Charles Cornwallis surrendered at Yorktown, Va., after which Britain began negotiating for an end to the war, even though she had won military control of the northern colonies.

1782

1 July. American privateers attacked Lunenburg, N.S.

9-24 August. On Hudson Bay, Fort Prince of Wales and York Fort surrendered to a French force under Jean-François de Galaup Comte de Laperouse.

30 November. Britain and the United States agreed on preliminary peace terms.

1783

18 May. 7,000 American Loyalists arrived at Parrtown (at the mouth of the Saint John River) as settlers.

3 September. The Treaty of Paris between Britain and the United States ended the American Revolution.

13 December. 30,000 Loyalists had reached Nova Scotia and New Brunswick.

1784

May-October. About 9,000 Loyalists settled in Ontario. They were allowed to go because the Iroquois wanted them settled nearby as a safeguard against American encroachment.

25 October. Governor Haldimand granted a tract of land along the Bay of Quinte and another on the Grand River to the Iroquois.

1788

John Meares arrived with two trading ships in Friendly Cove, Nootka Sound, and opened a trading post.

1789

5 May. Start of the Nootka Incident. The Spanish warship *Princesa* commanded by Estaban Martinez, arrived at Nootka to enforce Spain's claim to the west coast.

4 July. At Nootka, Martinez seized the British ship *Argonaut*

14 July. Martinez seized the British ship *Princess Royal*.

1790

10 April. Spain began erecting forts at Nootka.

24 July. Spain agreed to offer reparations to Britain for the seized ships.

28 October. The Nootka Convention was signed in Madrid. Spain agreed to give up claim to exclusive ownership of the west coast.

1792

Late September. Francisco de la Bodega y Quadra evacuated the Spanish base at Nootka Sound, although sovereignty had not been resolved.

1794

19 November. Jay's Treaty was signed. Britain agreed to evacuate the forts that were on United States territory in 1796.

1795

28 March. The Spanish evacuated their base at Friendly Cove, Nootka Sound.

1803

22 March. Massacre by Muquinna's Nootkas of 25 crew of the U.S. ship *Boston*, a trading vessel, in the Sound of Nootka. (Two survivors were rescued from the Indians in 1805.)

1807

22 December. United States passed the Embargo Act to stop all trade with foreign ports, in retaliation for Britain's Orders-in-Council and Napoleon's Decrees that interfered with American maritime rights.

1809

22 December. United States passed the Non-Intercourse Act which reopened trade to all nations except Britain and France.

1811

3 May. The Hudson's Bay Company agreed to sell Lord Selkirk 300,000 square kilometres (116,000 sq. mi.) for a colony at Red River.

1812

19 June. United States declared war on Britain.

A few days after the U.S. schooner *Julia* fought a naval engagement off Brockville with the British brig *Earl of Moira* and schooner *Duke of Gloucester*. The *Julia* took shelter in Ogdensburg harbour, and the other two retired to Kingston for repairs.

3 July. Capt. Frederic Rolette captured American Gen. William Hull's schooner *Cayahoga* and found Hull's battle plan.

12 July. Hull and 2,500 American troops occupied Sandwich.

17 July. A British party led by Capt. Charles Roberts captured Michilimackinac.

5 August. Indians led by Tecumseh cut Hull's supply line to Detroit.

8 August. Hull withdrew to Detroit.

13 August. Gen. Isaac Brock reached Amherstburg with 300 reinforcements from Toronto and Niagara.

14 August. Tecumseh and 600 Indians joined Brock to besiege Detroit.

15 August. The American garrison at Fort Dearborn (Chicago) was massacred by Indians.

16 August. Hull surrendered Detroit to Brock.

19-20 August. The U.S.S. *Constitution* defeated the British ship *Guerriere* off Nova Scotia.

1 September. Commodore Isaac Chauncey was appointed commander of American naval forces on the Great Lakes.

21 September. American riflemen led by Capt. Benjamin Forsyth raided Gananoque.

9 October. British ships *Detroit* and *Caledonia* were captured on Lake Erie by Capt. Jesse Elliot.

13 October. Battle of Queenston Heights. American troops under Gen. Stephen Van Rensselaer were defeated by a combined force of British, Canadians and Indians. Brock was killed in action, and Gen. Roger Sheaffe assumed command.

9-10 November. Gen. Henry Dearborn and 2,000 Americans attacked Odelltown (Que.), and were driven back to Lake Champlain by Col. Charles de Salaberry and his Canadian Voltigeurs.

22 January. Gen. Henry Proctor and 500 troops and 800 Indians under Tecumseh defeated the Americans at Frenchtown (Ohio).

7 February. Capt. Benjamin Forsyth and 200 riflemen raided Brockville and carried off 52 men.

22 February. A force led by Col. "Red George" Macdonell, captured the fort at Ogdensburg N.Y.

March. The 104th Regiment marched through the snow from Fredericton N.B. to Quebec City and lost only one man.

27 April. York, the capital of Upper Canada, was attacked by an American force under Gen. Zebulon Pike.

8 May. The Americans left York after burning the government buildings.

15 May. Capt. Sir James Yeo, R.N., took command of the Provincial Marine at Kingston.

27 May. Capture of Fort George, at Niagara, by Chauncey and Dearborn. The defenders, led by Gen. John Vincent, withdrew to Burlington Heights.

29 May. Yeo and Sheaffe attacked Sackets Harbor. The Americans, under Brigadier Jacob Brown, forced the British to withdraw.

1 June. H.M.S. *Shannon* captured the U.S.S. *Chesapeake* off Nova Scotia.

5-6 June. Battle of Stoney Creek. Gen. Vincent and Col. John Harvey defeated an American force under Brigadiers William Winder and John Chandler. The Americans withdrew to Forty Mile Creek.

8 June. Yeo's ships arrived at Forty Mile Creek and the Americans withdrew all the way to Fort George.

21-24 June. Battle of Beaver Dam. 570 Americans under Col. Charles Boerstler were ambushed by Lieut. James FitzGibbon with 50 regulars, and 400 Indians. 462 Americans were captured.

5-30 July. The British raided Fort Scholsser, Black Rock, and Plattsburgh N.Y.

10 September. Americans under Commodore Oliver Perry defeated a British naval force under Commodore Robert Barclay at Put-in Bay, Lake Erie.

18 September. American Gen. William H. Harrison forced Gen. Proctor to evacuate Detroit. Proctor moved up the Thames Valley accompanied by Tecumseh and his warriors.

6 October. Battle of Moraviantown. Harrison defeated Proctor, and Tecumseh was killed.

16 October. Sale of Fort Astoria (at the mouth of the Columbia River) by the Pacific Fur Company partners to partners of the North West Company. The fort was proclaimed British territory.

26 October. Battle of Chateauguay. Americans under Gen. Wade Hampton were defeated by Canadians under Col. Charles de Salaberry.

November. An American force of 8,000 men under Gen. James Wilkinson left Sackets Harbor expecting to link up with Gen. Hampton for a joint attack on Montreal.

11 November. Battle of Crysler's Farm. Wilkinson's subordiantes Brigadiers Boyd and Brown, were defeated in a rearguard action by Col. Joseph Morrison's regulars and Canadians.

30 November. Capt. William Black, R.N.,

arrived off the mouth of Columbia River in the armed sloop *Racoon*. On the 13 December. Black named Fort Astoria Fort George.

10 December. The American garrison evacuated Fort George (Niagara) and moved to Fort Niagara, N.Y. On the 11th they burned Newark (Niagara-on-the-Lake).

18 December. Col. John Murray and 500 British and Canadian troops captured Fort Niagara, N.Y.

18-30 December. Gen. Phineas Riall, with a party of Indians, burned Lewiston, Manchester, Fort Schlosser, Black Rock and Buffalo, N.Y.

1814

16-24 January. British troops raided Madrid, Salmon River, Malone and Four Corners, N.Y.

February. Americans raided Port Talbot (Ont).

30 March. Gen. James Wilkinson and 4,000 American troops, occupied Odelltown, Que., and were defeated by the British at Lacolle before they retreated to Plattsburgh.

6 May. Yeo captured Oswego and appropriated supplies.

15 May. 500 Americans raided, looted and burned Port Dover and Long Point, Lake Erie.

18 May. British reinforcements led by Col. Robert McDouall reached Michilmackinac to prevent the Americans from seizing it. In reserve were the Michigan Fencibles, commanded by William McKay, raised among Canadians living close to Lake Michigan.

20 May-6 June. The British blockaded Sackets Harbor.

30 May. Bateaux carrying British seamen went up Sandy Creek, off Lake Ontario near Sackets Harbor, to elude pursuing ships. The bateaux were ambushed by the Americans.

3 July. Brigadier Jacob Brown led American troops across the Niagara River to capture Fort Erie.

5 July. Battle of Chippawa. Brown's troops defeated Gen. Riall's 1,800-man force.

11 July. A British force from Halifax under Gen. Sir John Sherbrooke captured Eastport, Me., attacked Castine on 31 August. and Machias on 10 September. Eastern Maine was then in British hands.

18 July. 150 Michigan Fencibles under William McKay, and Indians from Green Bay, marched for the Mississippi. At Prairie-du-Chien (Iowa) they forced the U.S. gunboat *Governor Clark* to withdraw, and the garrison surrendered.

25 July. Battle of Lundy's Lane. Americans under Gen. Jacob Brown faced British and Canadians under Gen. Gordon Drummond. After heavy losses on both sides, the Americans withdrew, and the British claimed a victory.

4 August. At Michilimackinac a garrison of 200 under Col. Robert McDouall held off an attack by 750 Americans under Col. George Croghan.

14 August. The American ships *Niagara, Tigress* and *Scorpion* attacked the H.M.S. *Nancy* near Washaga Beach. Her commander, Lieut. Miller Worsley, burned her to prevent capture.

15 August. The British under Drummond began a siege of Fort Erie. Drummond was repulsed.

3 September. Lieut. Miller Worsley and 77 men in canoes captured the *Tigress*, at anchor northeast of Michilimackinac.

5 September. Using the *Tigress* and her American colours, Worsley captured the *Scorpion*.

10 September. The *St. Lawrence*, the largest wooden ship ever built on fresh water, was launched at Kingston.

11 September. Gen. Sir George Prevost was defeated on Lake Champlain by American Capt. Thomas Macdonough, and a British land force was repulsed from Plattsburgh.

October. The Americans lifted the blockade

of Kingston when the *St. Lawrence* was ready to sail.

5 November. The Americans destroyed Fort Erie and retired across the Niagara River.

24 December. The war ended with the signing of the Treaty of Ghent.

1815

15 June. Many of Selkirk's settlers left Red River out of fear of the fur traders.

25 June. Métis Cuthbert Grant attacked the fort at Red River, and the rest of the settlers left.

September. Colin Robertson and the Governor of the Hudson's Bay Company territories, George Semple, arrived at Red River to restore the settlement.

1816

19 June. Massacre of Seven Oaks. Cuthbert Grant's mounted column was escorting Red River carts full of pemmican when Governor Semple and 25 men went to intercept him. In the skirmish Semple and 19 of his men were killed.

13 August. Lord Selkirk led a private army of discharged veterans and captured Fort William, the headquarters of the North West Company. He arrested some of the partners and sent them to Montreal for trial for the massacre at Seven Oaks. Selkirk sent Miles Macdonell and 140 men to recapture Fort Douglas (headquarters of the Red River settlement) and Fort Daer (Pembina N.D.).

1817

28-29 April. The Rush-Bagot Agreement, limiting armaments on the Great Lakes, was signed in Washington D.C.

1818

20 October. Fort Astoria was restored to the Americans.

1819

22 February. By the Treaty of Florida Blanca, Spain gave up her claim to the Pacific coast north of the 42nd parallel.

1823

Work began on new fortifications for Quebec City (which were completed in 1832).

1824

18 May. William Lyon Mackenzie, the future rebel leader, published the first issue of his *Colonial Advocate*.

30 November. Construction began on the Welland Canal.

1826

8 June. Mackenzie's printing press at York was wrecked by Tory youths.

21 September. Work began on the Rideau Canal.

1827

6 August. In London, representatives of Britain and the United States agreed to continue co-dominion of the Pacific Northwest, with either country free to end the arrangement on 12 months notice.

24 September. The Talkotin and Chilkotin tribes on the upper Fraser River were at war. Hudson's Bay Company men gave the weaker Talkotins arms, and the Chilkotins withdrew.

1828

1 July. Alexander McLeod, chief trader of Fort Vancouver, led an attack on the lodge of the Challum Indians because they had murdered a Hudson's Bay Company clerk and his escort the previous January.

1829

27 November. The Welland Canal was completed to Port Robinson (and to Port Colborne in 1833).

1832

29 May. The steamer *Pumper* made the first trip through the Rideau Canal. (The Grenville and Carillon Canals, on the Ottawa River were completed in 1833, connecting Kingston with Montreal by an inland route safer than the St. Lawrence.)

Summer. Work began on the present Fort Henry at Kingston.

1834

17 February. The Lower Canada Assembly adopted the "Ninety-Two Resolutions".

27 March. Mackenzie became mayor of the

newly chartered City of Toronto.
18-29
June. Confrontation on the Stikene River between the Russians and Peter Skene Ogden on the Hudson's Bay Company ship *Dryad*. The Russians refused to let Ogden proceed upstream, and the *Dryad* withdrew.
1836
26 January. Sir John Colborne was appointed commander of forces in both the Canadas.
Late December. William Slacum, aboard the U.S. brig *Loriot* was spying in the Pacific Northwest. Afterwards the American settlers along the Columbia River opposed Hudson's Bay Company rule. Slacum sought to discredit Britain, and the United States determined to gain sovereignty over the west coast as far north as the 49th parallel.
1837
7 May. By the Declaration of St. Ours, Louis Joseph Papineau was chosen leader of the Lower Canadian *Patriotes*.
30 June. Mackenzie founded a Committee of Vigilance for Upper Canada.
October The 24th Regiment left Toronto, Kingston and Penetanguishene for Lower Canada at the request of Sir John Colborne.
6 November. *Patriote* Thomas Brown led the *Fils de la Liberté* in a street fight in Montreal against members of the Doric Club.
23 November. Battle of St. Denis. 2,000 British troops under Col. Charles Gore were defeated by *Patriotes* led by Wolfred Nelson.
25 November. Battle of St. Charles. Col. George Wetherall defeated the *Patriotes* after marching from Fort Chambly.
5 December. Mackenzie led 800 rebels down Yonge Street towards Toronto. His vanguard under Samuel Lount was dispersed by a picket posted at the edge of the city.
7 December. Volunteers under Col. James

FitzGibbon defeated Mackenzie's rebels near Montgomery's Tavern. Mackenzie fled to the United States.
13 December. Colborne defeated the *Patriotes* at St. Eustache.
15 December. *Patriotes* at St. Benôit surrendered to Colborne.
29 December. The American steamer *Caroline* was burnt in the Niagara River by Canadians under Capt. Andrew Drew.
1838
5 January. U.S. President Van Buren issued a Neutrality Proclamation forbidding U.S. citizens taking sides in the Canadian revolt.
26 February-3 March. Americans occupied Pelee Island, and were routed by British and Canadian troops led by Col. John Maitland.
28 February. A raid from Vermont into Lower Canada, led by Robert Nelson and Cyrille-Hector-Octave Coté, was dispersed by the milita.
30 March. Lord Durham was appointed governor general to investigate unrest in the Canadas.
29-30 May. Burning of the *Sir Robert Peel*. A gang led by Bill Johnston destroyed the steamer off Wellesley Island in the upper St. Lawrence River.
11-22 June. The Short Hills Raid. In Pelham Township, Niagara area, Americans and exiled Canadians were dispersed by the milita.
9 November. *Patriotes* who crossed from Vermont, led by Robert Nelson and Cyrille Coté, were dispersed at Lacolle and Odelltown.
11-16 November. Battle of the Windmill near Prescott (Ont.). 200 Americans and Canadian exiles occupied the windmill. After they surrendered, eleven were hanged at Kingston.
3 December. Battle of Windsor. American raiders were dispersed by militia and regulars.
10 December. The defeat of the *Patriotes*

who occupied the village of Beauharnois ended the second Lower Canadian Rebellion.

1839

4 February. Lord Durham submitted his report recommending the union of the Canadas.

All year. Indians of Bute Inlet, on the B.C. coast, were exterminated by the Yuculta Indians who lived along Johnstone Strait.

8 February. The "Aroostook War". Lumbermen of Maine and New Brunswick clashed because the border was not defined.

1840

23 July. The Act of Union of Upper and Lower Canada received Royal assent, to take effect 10 February 1841.

1842

American settlers on the Columbia River were calling for a U.S. boundary at 54 degrees, 40 minutes "or fight".

9 August. The Webster-Ashburton Treaty settled the boundary between Maine and New Brunswick.

1843

March. Fort Victoria, on Vancouver Island, was opened as the headquarters of the Hudson's Bay Company in the area.

1844

The Democratic candidate in the U.S. federal election, James Polk, campaigned on the slogan "Reoccupation of Oregon, Re-Annexation of Texas", although the U.S. had never owned either territory.

July. Cowichan Indians attacked Fort Victoria. Chief Trader Roderick Finlayson fired grape shot that shattered the Indians' nearby lodge, and a cannon ball that pierced a canoe in the harbour.

1846

15 June. The Oregon Boundary Treaty was signed. The boundary lay along the 49th parallel and the Strait of Juan de Fuca.

1856

29 January. The Victoria Cross was awarded to Alexander Dunn for gallantry at the Charge of the Light Brigade, the first Canadian to receive it.

1857

22 June. The Canadian Rifle Regiment was sent to Red River to counter American influence.

1861

8 November. The *Trent* Affair. U.S.S. *San Jacinto* stopped the British steamer *Trent* and seized two Confederate agents en route to Europe, which brought Britain and the United States to the brink of war.

30 December. The 62nd Regiment was sent to New Brunswick, the first of four regiments dispatched to Canada because of the *Trent* crisis.

1864

19 October. Confederate soldiers who had infiltrated Montreal raided St. Albans, Vt. and robbed banks of $90,000.

20 October. The Canadian militia was called out because of rumours of Fenian attacks.

1865

23 March. The British parliament voted £50,000 for Canadian defence after the Union ship *Kearsarge* sank the British-built Confederate ship *Alabama*.

1866

7 March. 10,000 Canadian militia were called out because of anticipated attacks by Fenians.

10 April. An attempt by Fenians to land on Campobello Island failed.

31 May.-2 June. Battle of Ridgeway. After crossing the Niagara River, Fenians led by John O'Neill defeated the Canadian militia at Ridgeway and withdrew to Fort Erie.

3 June. A relief force of British regulars and Canadian militia entered Fort Erie, but the Fenians had withdrawn towards the American side.

7 June. 1,000 Fenians crossed from Vermont into southern Quebec and plundered around Pigeon Hill, but retreated when the Canadian militia approached.

19 June. On a train filled with passengers and troops, Timothy O'Hea put out a fire before it could ignite gunpowder aboard. O'Hea was awarded the Victoria Cross, the only time it was given for valour within Canada.

1867

6 November. The new Parliament of Canada adopted a resolution for the entry of Rupert's Land and the Northwest Territory into Canada. (The Act for entry passed on 31 July 1868.)

1868

22 May. The first Dominion Militia Act was passed, but active units were not formed for three years.

1869

August. A government survey crew under John S. Dennis alarmed the Métis at Red River, who feared they would not be allowed to keep their lands.

11 October. A survey party at St. Vital, Man., was stopped by Louis Riel and 20 other Métis.

19 October. The Métis formed a National Committee at St. Norbert, Man., with Riel as secretary and John Bruce as president.

30 October. Métis refused to let William McDougall, the new Lieutenant Governor of Rupert's Land, enter the Red River colony.

2 November. Riel's Métis stormed Fort Garry (the site of Winnipeg), occupied it, formed a provisional government and proclaimed Riel its president.

26 November. Canada refused to take over Rupert's Land on 1 December as agreed because of Métis opposition. Prime Minister John A. Macdonald would not pay the Hudson's Bay Company for the land until McDougall could guarantee peaceful possession.

6 December. Governor General Lord Lisgar proclaimed a pardon if the Métis dispersed peacefully.

7 December. The Métis foiled an attempt by English-speaking Canadians to sieze

Fort Garry. Among them was Thomas Scott, an Oangeman from Ontario.

1870

January. Riel summoned a convention which agreed to form a provisional government to negotiate terms of entry into Confederation.

9 February. The Métis convention elected Riel president of Red River.

4 March. Thomas Scott was executed by firing squad, Riel's most serious blunder. Ontario viewed it as murder.

5 March. Britain and Canada agreed to a military expedition to Red River, and selected Col. Garnet Wolseley, the Deputy Quartermaster-General in Canada, to lead it.

May. The expedition, of the 60th Rifles and Ontario and Quebec militia units, prepared to move on Red River by way of Lake-of-the-Woods.

15 May. The Act establishing Manitoba as a province came into effect. 1,400,000 square miles (566,000 ha.) were set aside for the Métis.

25 May. Fenians under John O'Neill went to Eccles Hill, in southern Quebec, and were dispersed by the militia under Col. Osborn Smith.

15 July. The Hudson's Bay Company lands were annexed to Canada as the Northwest Territories.

24 August. Wolseley's expedition moved on Fort Garry. The Métis leaders fled and Riel reached the United States.

17 September. Riel made a secret visit to St. Norbert, Man. to persuade the Metis not to support Fenian invaders.

1871

5 October. Fenians under William B. O'Donoghue crossed the border into Manitoba and seized the Hudson's Bay Company post at Pembina. They were followed by American troops and arrested. Riel again returned in secret to assist the government.

11 November. The last British troops left

Quebec City, except for a small garrison that remained at Halifax.

1872

The Dominion Lands Act granted free homesteads to settlers in Manitoba. The influx of people dismayed the Métis, and many left to form new settlements on the Saskatchewan River.

January. The Ontario Legislature offered a reward of $5,000 for the capture of Louis Riel.

1873

Late May. The Cypress Hills Massacre. Ten American wolf hunters accused the Assiniboine Indians of stealing horses. In the fighting one wolfer and 36 Indians were killed.

23 May. An Act of Parliament set up the North West Mounted Police to keep peace between traders and Indians.

1876

1 June. Royal Military College opened in Kingston, to train officers for a Canadian regular army and the militia.

1884

5 June. Métis led by Gabriel Dumont visited Riel in Montana and he agreed to go to Saskatchewan and help them protect their rights from encroaching settlers.

8 July. Riel arrived at Duck Lake, on the North Saskatchewan River.

15 September. A force of 386 *voyageurs* under Col. Frederick Denison set sail for Egypt to assist in the rescue of Gen. Charles Gordon, then besieged at Khartoum, Sudan. Gen. Garnet Wolseley, who had commanded the expedition to Red River, asked for the *voyageurs* to help ascend the Nile. The expedition reached Khartoum on 28 January. 1885, but the city had fallen and Gordon was dead. This was Canada's first overseas military undertaking.

16 December. Riel's petition on Métis grievances was sent to Ottawa.

1885

January. The Canadian government agreed to form a commission to investigate Métis grievances.

11 March. From Fort Carlton, 32 km. from Batoche, N.W.M.P. Superintendent Leif Crozier warned Ottawa that rebellion was about to erupt in the Northwest.

18-19 May. At his headquarters at Batoche, Riel siezed hostages and proclaimed a Métis provisional government with himself as president, and Gabriel Dumont as adjutant-general.

21 March. Riel demanded the surrender of the N.W.M.P. detachment at Fort Carlton.

26 March. At Duck Lake the Métis defeated a detachment of N.W.M.P. led by Sup't Crozier.

30 March. Chief Poundmaker and 200 Crees attacked Battleford and the white settlers sought shelter at the N.W.M.P. barracks.

1 April. At Frog Lake, 9 whites and mixed bloods were murdered by Crees led by Wandering Spirit.

2 April. A three pronged expedition form the railway line was set in motion, under the overall command of Gen. Frederick Middleton, commander of the Canadian militia. Gen. Thomas Strange would go to Calgary and march for Edmonton; Col. William Otter would move north from Swift Current and relieve Battleford; Middleton would move north from Qu'Appelle towards Batoche.

15 April. N.W.M.P. Inspector Francis Dickens abandoned Fort Pitt after white civilians under his protection decided to surrender to Big Bear.

24 April. Middleton's force was badly mauled at Fish Creek. On the same day, Otter relieved Battleford.

2-3 May. At Cut Knife Hill, Otter's force withdrew after meeting stiff resistance from Poundmaker's Crees.

9-12 May. Battle of Batoche. The government forces broke Métis resistance decisively. Riel surrendered on 15 May. Dumont escaped and reached the United States.

25 May. Poundmaker surrendered to
Middleton near Battleford.
27-28 May. At Frenchman's Butte, Alta.,
Big Bear retreated from Strange's force.
3 June. Steele Narrows – the last battle on
Canadian soil. A detachment of N.W.M.P.
under Samuel Steele fought with Crees
under Big Bear, but the Cree chief escaped.
2 July. Big Bear surrendered at Fort
Carlton.
16 November. Riel was hanged at the
N.W.M.P. barracks in Regina.
27 November. Wandering Spirit and 7
other Indians were hanged for the murders
committed at Frog Lake in April.

Suggested Further Reading

Chapter 1. Huronia

Cranston, J. Herbert. *Huronia*. Minesing, Ont. 1969. Huronia Historic Sites Association.

Marquis, Thomas Guthrie. *The Jesuit Missions*. Toronto 1920. Chronicles of Canada, vol. 4.

Chapter 2. Louisbourg

Downey, Fairfax *Louisbourg: Key to a Continent*. Englewood, N.J. 1965.

McLennan, J.S. *Louisbourg From its Foundation to its Fall*. Sydney 1969. First published in 1918.

Chapter 3. Beauséjour

Stanley, George F.G. *New France: the Last Phase 1744-1760*. Toronto 1968.

Chapter 4. Carillon

Leach, Douglas Edward. *Arms for Empire: a Military History of the British Colonies in North America 1607-1763*. New York 1973.

Chapter 5. Quebec

Grinnell-Milne, Duncan. *Mad, is He? The Character and Achievements of James Wolfe*. London 1963.

Stacey, C. J. *Quebec 1759: the Siege and the Battle*. Toronto 1959.

Chapter 6. Thousand Islands

Fryer, Mary B. and Ten Cate, A.G. *Pictorial History of the Thousand Islands. Brockville 1982*.

Snider, C.H.J. *Tarry Breeks and Velvet Garters*. Toronto 1958.

Chapter 7. Signal Hill

Candow, James E. "A History of Signal Hill." Parks Canada, Atlantic Regional Office 1981. Unpublished paper.

Chapter 8. St. Jean

Fryer, Mary B. *King's Men: the Soldier Founders of Ontario*. Toronto 1980.

Stanley, George F.G. *Canada Invaded 1775-1776* National Museum of Man 1973. Canadian War Museum Historical Publication No. 8.

Chapter 9. Nootka

Kendrick, John. *The Men with Wooden Feet: The Spanish Exploration of the Pacific Northwest*. Toronto 1986

Chapter 10. Queenston Heights

Stanley, George F.G. *The War of 1812: Land Operations*. National Museum of Man 1983. Canadian War Museum Historical Publication No. 18.

Chapter 11. Stoney Creek

Hitsman, J. Mackay, *The Incredible War of 1812*. Toronto 1965.

Chapter 12. Chateauguay

Wohler, J. Patrick *Charles de Salaberry: Soldier of the Empire, Defender of Quebec*. Toronto 1984. Dundurn Lives Series.

Chapter 13. St. Charles

Senior, Elinor Kyte *Redcoats and Patriotes: The Rebellions in Lower Canada 1837-38*. National Museum of Man 1985. Canadian War Museum Historical Publication No. 20.

Chapter 14. Windmill Point

Flemming, David *Battle of the Windmill, 1838*. Parks Canada, National and Historic Sites Branch, History and Archaeology Publication No. 8. 1976.

Pipping, Ella. *Soldier of Fortune* Toronto 1968.

Chapter 15. Ridgeway

Macdonald, Capt. John A. *Troublous Times in Canada: a History of the Fenian Raids in 1866 and 1870*. Toronto 1910.

Chapter 16. Batoche

Morton, Desmond. *The Last War Drum: the North West Campaign of 1885*. National Museum of Man 1972. Canadian War Museum Historical Publication, unnumbered.

Illustration, Photograph and Map Credits

Maps by Mary Beacock Fryer and Andy Tong

Illustrations and Photographs

Abbreviations

JRR: John Ross Robertson Collection, MTL
MTL: Metropolitan Toronto Library
OA: Ontario Archives
PAC: Public Archives of Canada
PANL: Public Archives of Newfoundland and Labrador

Page Source

12 PAC S750
15 Ontario Department of Tourism and Information, *Historic Ontario*,36
19 PAC C1048
20 McGill University Libraries
21 Ontario Ministry of Tourism and Information
23 PAC C2077
26 PAC C4816
31 PAC C5907
36 France, Bibliothèque Nationale, Maps and Plans GeC5019
37 National Maritime Museum, London, Visual Indes no.1770
38 Top: France, AN Outremer, D.F.C., carton IV, no. 158
    Bottom: Parks Canada, Louisbourg National Historic Park
41 Eglise Saint-Sauveur de la Rochelle, Cliché Giraudon, LA 17559
44 Parks Canada, Louisbourg National Historic Park
47 PAC C19938
51 PAC H4/205
52 PAC C9506
54 Parks Canada, Beauséjour National Historic Park
55 Top: Parks Canada, Beauséjour National Historic Park
    Bottom: Painting by Dusan Kadlec in the possession of Enviornment Canada, Parks, Atlantic
    Region
56 Painting by Dusan Kadlec in the possession of Enviornment Canada, Parks, Atlantic Region
57 Fort Ticonderoga Museum, Ticonderoga, N.Y.
59 PAC, from a sketch by Thomas Davies
64 Fort Ticonderoga Museum, Ticonderoga N.Y.
65 Fort Ticonderoga Museum, Ticonderoga N.Y.
66 Fort Ticonderoga Museum, Ticonderoga N.Y.
67 MTL JRR
72 PAC C118259
75 OA S1671
78 PAC C1078
82 PAC
83 PAC C37
87 PAC, redrawn by F.C. Curry
89 Sketch by John C. Lamontagne
90 Sketch by John C. Lamontagne
92 PAC Map Division, unnumbered, courtesy of Adrian G.TenCate
93 National Gallery of Canada
95 Sketch by John C. Lamontagne
96 PAC, redrawn by F. C. Curry, copy in the Brockville Museum
97 PAC, redrawn by F. C. Curry, copy in the Brockville Museum
98 Photograph by Dennis Wallace
104 PANL B2-128
105 PAC C3371
107 PANL B3-129
110 John Carter Brown Library, Brown University, Providence R.I.
111 MTL JRR
113 Parks Canada, Fort Chambly National Historic Park
115 New York Public Library, Prints Divsion
117 Jack Coggins, *Ships and Seamen of the American Revolution*
118 National Galleries of Scotland

119 MTL JRR
120 Fort Ticonderoga Museum, Ticonderoga, N.Y.
122 Lord Maclean of Duart and Morvern
124 Fort Ticonderoga Museum, Ticonderoga, N.Y.
125 Top: PAC, from an aquatint by Col. J. Bouchette
    Bottom:PAC, from a contemporary lithograph
128 PAC C4730
131 PAC C17726
134 Vancouver Public Library
135 Museo Naval de Madrid
136 Vancouver Public Library
139 Pohotgraph by Cathie Archbould
141 Vancouver Public Library
142 OA S1439
146 PAC C7756
149 PAC 18775
153 OA S1440
154 MTL JRR
155 PAC
156 Artist unknown, from *Harper's Weekly*, 16 June 1866
157 Niagara Parks Commission, Battlefield House collection

160 MTL, portrait by A Buck
161 Niagara Parks Commission, Battlefield House collection
162 Niagara Parks Commission, Battlefield House collection
164 Niagara Parks Commission, Battlefield House collection
168 Chateau Ramezay Museum, Montreal, portrait by Don G. McNab
171 Parks Canada, sketch by Eugene Lelièpvre
175 Top: Sketch from an illustration by David Thompson
    Bottom: Photograph by Judy Wohler
176 Photograph by Judy Wohler
178 PAC C11240
183 PAC C11856
184 PAC C395
186 PAC C394
188 Chateau Ramezay Museum, photo by Giles Rivest
193 MTL JRR T16107
195 PAC from Lossing's book on the War of 1812
197 MTL JRR
198 MTL JRR T16112
199 MTL JRR
201 OA S13289
203 MTL JRR T15422
204 MTL JRR T16390
206 PAC C18737
209 OA S2865
214 from Gauust Doscen's history of the Fenian raids
215 from Gauust Doscen's history of the Fenian raids
219 property of the author
222 PAC
225 National Film Board
229 PAC
231 Top: PAC C7684
    Bottom: PAC C7681
232 Batoche National Historic Park
240 PAC, print by J. Lecomte

Index

Illustrations are in bold type

Ships' names are in italics